THE
NEGRO
SOLDIER

A Select Compilation

NEGRO UNIVERSITIES PRESS
NEW YORK

Originally published in 1861
by R.F. Wallcut, Boston

Reprinted in 1970 by
Negro Universities Press
A Division of Greenwood Press, Inc.
Westport, Connecticut

Library of Congress Catalogue Card Number 68-55925

SBN 8371-1870-0

Printed in United States of America

CONTENTS

THE

LOYALTY AND DEVOTION

OF

COLORED AMERICANS

IN THE

REVOLUTION AND WAR OF 1812.

BOSTON:

PATRIOTISM OF COLORED AMERICANS.

At a Mass Convention of the colored citizens of Ohio, held at Cleveland, Sept. 9th, 1852, the orator of the occasion, William H. Day, Esq., in the course of his address, said : —

" ' Of the services and sufferings of the colored soldiers of the Revolution,' says one writer, ' no attempt has, to our knowledge, been made to preserve a record.' This is mainly true. Their history is not written. It lies upon the soil watered with their blood: who shall gather it? It rests with their bones in the charnel-house : who shall exhume it? Their bodies, wrapped in sacks, have dropped from the decks where trod a Decatur and a Barry, in a calm and silence broken only by the voice of the man of God — ' We commit this body to the deep;' and the plunge and the ripples passing, the sea has closed over their memory forever. Ah! we have waited on shore and have seen the circle of that ripple. We know, at least, where they went down; and so much, to-day, we come to record.

" We have had in Ohio, until very recently, and if they are living, have here now, a few colored men who have thus connected us with the past. I have been told of one, recently, in the southern portion of the State.

" Another, of whom we all know, has resided, for many years, near Urbana, Champagne county. He was invited to, and expected at, this meeting. Father Stanup (as he is familiarly called) has lived to a good old age. He has been afflicted with recent sickness, and it may have prostrated him permanently. The frosts of a hundred winters will shrivel any oak; the blasts of a century will try *any* vitality. The aged soldier must soon die. O, that liberty, for which he fought, might be bequeathed to his descendants! The realization of that idea would smooth his dying pillow, and make the transit from this to another sphere a pleasant passage. I am credibly informed, that the age of Mr. Stanup is one hundred and nine; that he was with General Washington; and that his position, in this respect, has been recognized by officers of the Government."

Further on, Mr. Day said: — "I think we have demonstrated this point, that if colored people are among your Pompeys, and Cuffees, and Uncle Toms, they are also among your heroes. They have been on Lakes Erie and Champlain, upon the Mediterranean, in Florida with the Creeks, at Schuylkill, at Hickory Ground, at New Orleans, at Horse Shoe Bend, and at Pensacola. The presence of some of them here to-day is a living rebuke to this land."

Addressing the large crowd of white citizens present, Mr. Day said: — "We can be, as we have always been, faithful subjects, powerful allies, as the documents read here to-day prove: an enemy in your midst, we would be more powerful still. We ask for liberty; liberty here — liberty on the Chalmette Plains — liberty wherever floats the American flag. We demand for the sons of the men who fought for you, equal privileges. We bring to you, to-day, the tears of our fathers, — each tear is a volume, and speaks to you. To you, then, we appeal. We point you to their blood, sprinkled upon your door-posts in your political midnight, that the Destroying Angel might pass over. We take you to their sepulchres, to see the bond of honor between you and them kept, on their part, faithfully, even until death."

The following extracts from an address delivered, in 1842, before the Congregational and Presbyterian Anti-Slavery Society, at Francestown, N. H., by Dr. Harris, a Revolutionary veteran, will be read with great interest: —

"I sympathize deeply," said Dr. Harris, "in the objects of this Society. I fought, my hearers, for the liberty which you enjoy. It surprises me that every man does not rally at the sound of liberty, and array himself with those who are laboring to abolish slavery in our country. The very mention of it warms the blood in my veins, and, old as I am, makes me feel something of the spirit and impulses of '76.

" *Then* liberty meant something. Then liberty, independence, freedom, were in every man's mouth. They were the sounds at which they rallied, and under which they fought and bled. They were the words which encouraged and cheered them through their hunger, and nakedness, and fatigue, in cold and in heat. The word slavery then filled their hearts with horror. They fought because they would not be slaves. Those whom liberty has cost nothing, do not know how to prize it.

" I served in the Revolution, in General Washington's army, three years under one enlistment. I have stood in battle where balls, like hail, were flying all around me. The man standing next to me was shot by my side—his blood spouted upon my clothes, which I wore for weeks. My nearest blood, except that which runs in my veins, was shed for liberty. My only brother was shot dead instantly in the Revolution. Liberty is dear to my heart; I cannot endure the thought that my countrymen should be slaves.

" When stationed in the State of Rhode Island, the regiment to which I belonged was once ordered to what was called a flanking position,—that is, upon a place which the enemy must pass in order to come round in our rear, to drive us from the fort. This pass was every thing, both to them and to us; of course, it was a post of imminent danger. They attacked us with great fury, but were repulsed. They reinforced, and attacked us again, with more vigor and determination, and again were repulsed. Again they reinforced, and attacked us the third time, with the most desperate courage and resolution, but a third time were repulsed. The contest was fearful. Our position was hotly disputed and as hotly maintained.

"But I have another object in view in stating these facts. I would not be trumpeting my own acts; the only reason why I have named myself in connection with this transaction is, to show that I know whereof I affirm. There was a *black* regiment in the same situation. Yes, a regiment of *negroes*, fighting for *our* liberty and independence,—not a white man among them but the officers,—stationed in this same danger-

ous and responsible position. Had they been unfaithful, or
given way before the enemy, all would have been lost. *Three
times in succession* were they attacked, with most desperate
valor and fury, by well disciplined and veteran troops, and
three times did they successfully repel the assault, and thus
preserve our army from capture. They fought through the
war. They were brave, hardy troops. They helped to gain
our liberty and independence.

"Now, the war is over, our freedom is gained — what is to
be done with these colored soldiers, who have shed their best
blood in its defence? Must they be sent off out of the country, because they are black? or must they be sent back into
slavery, now they have risked their lives and shed their blood
to secure the freedom of their masters? I ask, what became
of these noble colored soldiers? Many of them, I fear, were
taken back to the South, and doomed to the fetter and the
chain.

"And why is it, that the colored inhabitants of our nation,
born in this country, and entitled to all the rights of freemen,
are held in slavery? Why, but because they are *black?*
I have often thought that, should God see fit, by a miracle, to
change their color, straighten their hair, and give their features and complexion the appearance of the whites, slavery
would not continue a year. No, you would then go and
abolish it with the *sword*, if it were not speedily done without. But is it a suitable cause for making men slaves, because God has given them such a color, such hair and such
features, as he saw fit?"

Dr. Clarke, in the Convention which revised the Constitution of New York, in 1821, speaking of the colored inhabitants of the State, said: —

"My honorable colleague has told us, that, as the colored
people are not required to contribute to the protection or defence of the State, they are not entitled to an equal participation in the privileges of its citizens. But, Sir, whose fault
is this? Have they ever refused to do military duty when
called upon? It is haughtily asked, Who will stand in the
ranks shoulder to shoulder with a negro? I answer, No one,
in time of peace; no one, when your musters and trainings

are looked upon as mere pastimes; no one, when your militia will shoulder their muskets and march to their trainings with as much unconcern as they would go to a sumptuous entertainment or a splendid ball. But, Sir, when the hour of danger approaches, your white 'militia' are just as willing that the man of color should be set up as a mark to be shot at by the enemy, as to be set up themselves. In the War of the Revolution, these people helped to fight your battles by land and by sea. Some of your States were glad to turn out corps of colored men, and to stand 'shoulder to shoulder' with them.

"In your late war, they contributed largely towards some of your most splendid victories. On Lakes Erie and Champlain, where your fleets triumphed over a foe superior in numbers and engines of death, they were manned, in a large proportion, with men of color. And, in this very house, in the fall of 1814, a bill passed, receiving the approbation of all the branches of your government, authorizing the Governor to accept the services of a corps of two thousand free people of color. Sir, these were times which tried men's souls. In these times, it was no sporting matter to bear arms. These were times, when a man who shouldered his musket did not know but he bared his bosom to receive a death wound from the enemy ere he laid it aside; and, in these times, these people were found as ready and as willing to volunteer in your service as any other. They were not compelled to go; they were not drafted. No; your pride had placed them beyond your compulsory power. But there was no necessity for its exercise; they were volunteers; yes, Sir, volunteers to defend that very country from the inroads and ravages of a ruthless and vindictive foe, which had treated them with insult, degradation and slavery.

"Volunteers are the best of soldiers. Give me the men, whatever be their complexion, that willingly volunteer, and not those who are compelled to turn out. Such men do not fight from necessity, nor from mercenary motives, but from principle."

The Hon. Tristam Burges, of Rhode Island, in a speech in Congress, January, 1828, said:—"At the commencement of the Revolutionary War, Rhode Island had a number of slaves. A regiment of them were enlisted into the Continental service, and no braver men met the enemy in battle; but not one of them was permitted to be a soldier until he had first been made a freeman."

"In Rhode Island," says Governor Eustis, in his able speech against slavery in Missouri, 12th December, 1820, "the blacks formed an entire regiment, and they discharged their duty with zeal and fidelity. The gallant defence of Red Bank, in which the black regiment bore a part, is among the proofs of their valor."

In this contest, it will be recollected that four hundred men met and repulsed, after a terrible and sanguinary struggle, fifteen hundred Hessian troops, headed by Count Donop. The glory of the defence of Red Bank, which has been pronounced one of the most heroic actions of the war, belongs in reality to black men; yet who now hears them spoken of in connection with it? Among the traits which distinguished the black regiment was devotion to their officers. In the attack made upon the American lines, near Croton river, on the 13th of May, 1781, Col. Greene, the commander of the regiment, was cut down and mortally wounded; but the sabres of the enemy only reached him through the bodies of his faithful guard of blacks, who gathered around him to protect him, *and every one of whom was killed.*

The celebrated Charles Pinckney, of South Carolina, in his speech on the Missouri question, and in defence of the slave representation of the South, made the following admissions: —

"At the commencement of our Revolutionary struggle with Great Britain, all the States had this class of people. The New England States had numbers of them; the Northern and Middle States had still more, although less than the Southern. *They all entered into the great contest with similar views. Like brethren, they contended for the benefit of the whole,* leaving to each the right to pursue its happiness in its own way. They thus nobly toiled and bled together, *really like brethren.* And it is a remarkable fact, that, notwithstanding, in the course of the Revolution, the Southern States were continually overrun by the British, and every negro in them had an opportunity of running away, yet few did. They then were, as they still are, as valuable a part of our population to the Union as any other equal number of inhabitants. They were in numerous instances the pioneers, and in all, the laborers of your armies. *To their hands were owing the erection of the greatest part of the fortifications raised for the protection of our country.* Fort Moultrie gave, at an early period of the inexperience and untried valor of our citizens, immortality to American arms. And in the Northern States, numerous bodies of them were enrolled, and fought, *side-by-side with the whites,* the battles of the Revolution."

Said Martindale, of New York, in Congress, 22d of January, 1828 : — "Slaves, or negroes who had been slaves, were enlisted as soldiers in the War of the Revolution ; and I myself saw a battalion of them, as fine martial-looking men as I ever saw, attached to the Northern army, in the last war, on its march from Plattsburg to Sackett's Harbor."

The Burlington *Gazette* gives the following account of an aged colored resident of that city, which will be read with much interest : —

"The attention of many of our citizens has, doubtless, been arrested by the appearance of an old colored man, who might have been seen, sitting in front of his residence, in East Union street, respectfully raising his hat to those who might be passing by. His attenuated frame, his silvered head, his feeble movements, combine to prove that he is very aged; and yet, comparatively few are aware that he is among the survivors of the gallant army who fought for the liberties of our country, 'in the days which tried men's souls.'

"On Monday last, we stopped to speak to him, and asked him how old he was. He asked the day of the month, and, upon being told that it was the 24th of May, replied, with trembling lips, 'I am very old — I am a hundred years old to-day.'

"His name is Oliver Cromwell, and he says that he was born at the Black Horse, (now Columbus,) in this county, in the family of John Hutchin. He enlisted in a company commanded by Capt. Lowery, attached to the Second New

1*

Jersey Regiment, under the command of Col. Israel Shreve. He was at the battles of Trenton, Princeton, Brandywine, Monmouth, and Yorktown, at which latter place, he told us, he saw the last man killed. Although his faculties are failing, yet he relates many interesting reminiscences of the Revolution. He was with the army at the retreat of the Delaware, on the memorable crossing of the 25th of December, 1776, and relates the story of the battles on the succeeding days with enthusiasm. He gives the details of the march from Trenton to Princeton, and told us, with much humor, that they 'knocked the British about lively' at the latter place. He was also at the battle of Springfield, and says that he saw the house burning in which Mrs. Caldwell was shot, at Connecticut Farms."

I further learn, (says the author of "The Colored Patriots of the Revolution,") that Cromwell was brought up a farmer, having served his time with Thomas Hutchins, Esq., his maternal uncle. He was, for six years and nine months, under the immediate command of Washington, whom he loved affectionately. "His discharge," says Dr. M'Cune Smith, "at the close of the war, was in Washington's own hand-writing, of which he was very proud, often speaking of it. He received, annually, ninety-six dollars pension. He lived a long and honorable life. Had he been of a little lighter complexion, (he was just half white,) every newspaper in the land would have been eloquent in praise of his many virtues."

Jack Grove, of Portland, while steward of a brig, sailing from the West Indies to Portland, in 1812, was taken by a French vessel, whose commander placed a guard on board. Jack urged his commander to make an effort to retake the vessel, but the captain saw no hope. Says Jack, "Captain McLellan, I can take her, if you will let me go ahead." The captain checked him, warning him not to lisp such a word, — there was danger in it; but Jack, disappointed, though not daunted, rallied the men on his own hook. Captain McLellan and the rest, inspired by his example, finally joined them, and the attempt resulted in victory. They weighed anchor, and took the vessel into Portland.

FORMATION OF A COLORED REGIMENT IN RHODE ISLAND.

STATE OF RHODE ISLAND AND PROVIDENCE PLANTATIONS, IN GENERAL ASSEMBLY. February Session, 1778.

Whereas, for the preservation of the rights and liberties of the United States, it is necessary that the whole power of Government should be exerted in recruiting the Continental battalions; and, whereas, His Excellency, General Washington, hath inclosed to this State a proposal made to him by Brigadier General Varnum, to enlist into the two battalions raising by this State such slaves as should be willing to enter into the service; and, whereas, history affords us frequent precedents of the wisest, the freest and bravest nations having liberated their slaves and enlisted them as soldiers to fight in defence of their country; and also, whereas, the enemy have, with great force, taken possession of the capital and ot a great part of this State, and this State is obliged to raise a very considerable number of troops for its own immediate defence, whereby it is in a manner rendered impossible for this State to furnish recruits for the said two battalions without adopting the said measures so recommended, —

It is Voted and Resolved, That every able-bodied negro, mulatto, or Indian man-slave in this State may enlist into either of the said two battalions, to serve during the continuance of the present war with Great Britain; —That every slave so enlisting shall be entitled to and receive all the bounties, wages and encouragements allowed by the Continental Congress to any soldiers enlisting into this service.

It is further Voted and Resolved, That every slave so enlisting shall, upon his passing muster by Col. Christopher Greene, be immediately discharged from the service of his master or mistress, and be absolutely free, as though he had never been incumbered with any kind of servitude or slavery. And in case such slave shall, by sickness or otherwise, be rendered unable to maintain himself, he shall not be chargeable to his master or mistress, but shall be supported at the expense of the State.

And, whereas, slaves have been by the laws deemed the property of their owners, and therefore compensation ought to be made to the owners for the loss of their service, —

It is further Voted and Resolved, That there be allowed and paid by this State to the owners, for every such slave so enlisting, a sum according to his worth, at a price not exceeding one hundred and twenty pounds for the most valuable slave, and in proportion for a slave of less value,—provided the owner of said slave shall deliver up to the officer who shall enlist him the clothes of the said slave, or otherwise he shall not be entitled to said sum.

And for settling and ascertaining the value of such slaves,—It is further Voted and Resolved, That a committee of five shall be appointed, to wit,—one from each county, any three of whom to be a quorum,—to examine the slaves who shall be so enlisted, after they shall have passed muster, and to set a price upon each slave, according to his value as aforesaid.

It is further Voted and Resolved, That upon any able-bodied negro, mulatto or Indian slave enlisting as aforesaid, the officer who shall so enlist him, after he has passed muster as aforesaid, shall deliver a certificate thereof to the master or mistress of said negro, mulatto, or Indian slave, which shall discharge him from the service of said master or mistress.

It is further Voted and Resolved, That the committee who shall estimate the value of the slave aforesaid, shall give a certificate of the sum at which he may be valued to the owner of said slave, and the general treasurer of this State is hereby empowered and directed to give unto the owner of said slave his promissory note for the sum of money at which he shall be valued as aforesaid, payable on demand, with interest,—which shall be paid with the money from Congress.

A true copy, examined,

HENRY WARD, *Sec'y.*

Among the brave blacks who fought in the battles for American liberty was Major Jeffrey, a Tennesseean, who, during the campaign of Major-General Andrew Jackson in Mobile, filled the place of "regular" among the soldiers. In the charge made by General Stump against the enemy, the Americans were repulsed and thrown into disorder,—Major Stump being forced to retire, in a manner by no means desirable, under the circumstances. Major Jeffrey, who was but a common soldier, seeing the condition of his comrades, and comprehending the disastrous results about to befall them, rushed forward, mounted a horse, took command of the troops, and, by an heroic effort, rallied them to the charge, — completely routing the enemy, who left the Americans masters of the field. He at once received from the General the title of "Major," though he could not, according to the American policy, so commission him. To the day of his death, he was known by that title in Nashville, where he resided, and the circumstances which entitled him to it were constantly the subject of popular conversation.

Major Jeffrey was highly respected by the whites generally, and revered, in his own neighborhood, by all the colored people who knew him.

A few years ago, receiving an indignity from a common ruffian, he was forced to strike him in self-defence; for which act, in accordance with the laws of slavery in that, as well as many other of the slave States, he was compelled to receive, on his naked person, *nine and thirty lashes with a raw hide!* This, at the age of seventy odd, after the distinguished services rendered his country, — probably when the white ruffian for whom he was tortured was unable to raise an arm in its defence, — was more than he could bear; *it broke his heart*, and he sank to rise no more, till summoned by the blast of the last trumpet to stand on the battle-field of the general resurrection.

Lieutenant-Colonel Barton, of the Rhode Island militia, planned a bold exploit for the purpose of surprising and taking Major-General Prescott, the commanding officer of the royal army at Newport. Taking with him, in the night, about forty men, in two boats, with oars muffled, he had the address to elude the vigilance of the ships of war and guard boats, and, having arrived undiscovered at the General's quarters, they were taken for the sentinels, and the General was not alarmed till his captors were at the door of his lodging chamber, which was fast closed. A negro man, named Prince, instantly thrust his head through the panel door, and seized the victim while in bed. The General's aid-de-camp leaped from a window undressed, and attempted to escape, but was taken, and, with the General, brought off in safety.*

* Thacher's Military Journal, August 3, 1777.

Swett, in his "Sketches of Bunker Hill Battle," alludes to the presence of a colored man in that fight. He says: — "Major Pitcairn caused the first effusion of blood at Lexington. In that battle, his horse was shot under him, while he was separated from his troops. With presence of mind, he feigned himself slain; his pistols were taken from his holsters, and he was left for dead, when he seized the opportunity, and escaped. He appeared at Bunker Hill, and, says the historian, ' Among those who mounted the works was the gallant Major Pitcairn, who exultingly cried out, " *The day is ours!* " when a black soldier named Salem shot him through, and he fell. His agonized son received him in his arms, and tenderly bore him to the boats.' A contribution was made in the army for the colored soldier, and he was presented to Washington as having performed this feat."

Besides Salem, there were quite a number of colored soldiers at Bunker Hill. Among them, Titus Coburn, Alexander Ames, and Barzilai Lew, all of Andover; and also Cato Howe, of Plymouth — each of whom received a pension.

Samuel Charlton was born in the State of New Jersey, a slave, in the family of Mr. M., who owned, also, other members belonging to his family — all residing in the English neighborhood. During the progress of the war, he was placed by his master (as a substitute for himself) in the army then in New Jersey, as a teamster in the baggage train. He was in active service at the battle of Monmouth, not only witnessing, but taking a part in, the struggle of that day. He was also in several other engagements in different sections of that part of the State. He was a great admirer of General Washington, and was, at one time, attached to his baggage train, and received the General's commendation for his courage and devotion to the cause of liberty. Mr. Charlton was about fifteen or seventeen years of age when placed in the army, for which his master rewarded him with a silver dollar. At the expiration of his time, he returned to his master, to serve again in bondage, after having toiled, fought and bled for liberty, in common with the regular soldiery. Mr. M., at his death, by will, liberated his slaves, and provided a pension for Charlton, to be paid during his lifetime.

Quack Matrick, of Stoughton Corner, was a regular Revolutionary soldier, and drew a pension.

In the engravings of Washington crossing the Delaware, o the evening previous to the battle of Trenton, Dec. 25th, 1779, a colored soldier is seen, on horseback, quite prominent, near the Commander-in-Chief, — the same figure that, in other sketches, is seen pulling the stroke oar in that memorable crossing. This colored soldier was Prince Whipple, body-guard to Gen. Whipple, of New Hampshire, who was Aid to General Washington.

The names of the two brave men of color who fell, with Ledyard, at the storming of Fort Griswold, were Lambo Latham and Jordan Freeman. When Major Montgomery, one of the leaders in the expedition against the Americans, was lifted upon the walls of the fort by his soldiers, flourishing his sword and calling on them to follow him, Jordan Freeman received him on the point of a pike, and pinned him dead to the earth.

Ebenezer Hills died at Vienna, New York, August, 1849, aged one hundred and ten. He was born a slave, in Stonington, Connecticut, and became free when twenty-eight years of age. He served through the Revolutionary War, and was at the battles of Saratoga and Stillwater, and was present at the surrender of Burgoyne.

In Washington's Will, special provision is made for his " mulatto man William, calling himself William Lee," granting him his immediate freedom, an annuity of thirty dollars during his natural life, or support, if he preferred (being incapable of walking or any active employment) to remain with the family. " This I give him," says Washington, " as a testimony of my sense of his attachment to me, and for *his faithful services during the Revolutionary War.*"

Simon Lee, the grandfather of William Wells Brown, on his mother's side, was a slave in Virginia, and served in the War of the Revolution. Although honorably discharged, with the other Virginia troops, at the close of the war, he was sent back to his master, where he spent the remainder of his life toiling on a tobacco plantation.

Jonathan Overton, (says the Edenton *Whig*,) a colored man, and a soldier of the Revolution, died at this place, at the advanced age of one hundred and one years. The deceased served under Washington, and was at the battle of Yorktown, besides other less important engagements. He was deservedly held in great respect by our citizens; for, apart from the feeling of veneration which every American must entertain for the scanty remnant of Revolutionary heroes, of which death is fast depriving us, the deceased was personally worthy of the esteem and consideration of our community. He has lived among us longer than the ordinary period allotted to human life, and always sustained a character for honesty, industry, and integrity.

James Easton, of Bridgewater, a colored man, participated in the erection of the fortifications on Dorchester Heights, under command of Washington, which the next morning so greatly surprised the British soldiers then encamped in Boston.

Job Lewis, of Lancaster, (formerly a slave,) enlisted for two terms of three years each; and a third time for the remainder of the war. He died in November, 1797.

Prince Richards, of East Bridgewater, was a pensioned Revolutionary soldier.

Thomas Hollen, of Dorset county, Maryland, was in the Revolutionary War, attached to the regiment of Col. Charles Gouldsbury, and was wounded by a musket ball in the calf of his leg. He died in 1816, aged seventy two, at the town of Blackwood, N. J., and was buried in the Snowhill churchyard, east of Woodbury.

The Legislature of Virginia, in 1783, emancipated several slaves who had fought in the Revolutionary War, and the example was followed by some individuals, who wished to exhibit a consistency of conduct rare even in those early days of our country's history. The Baltimore papers of September 8th, 1790, make mention of the fact that Hon. General Gates, before taking his departure, with his lady, for their new and elegant seat on the banks of the East River, summoned his numerous family and slaves about him, and, amidst their tears of affection and gratitude, gave them their freedom; and, what was still better, made provision that their liberty should be a blessing to them.

During the Revolutionary War, the Legislature of New York passed an Act granting freedom to all slaves who should serve in the army for three years, or until regularly discharged. (See 1 Kent's Com., p. 255.)

Rev. Theodore Parker, in a letter to the author of "The Colored Patriots of the American Revolution," says : —

"Not long ago, while the excavations for the vaults of the great retail dry goods store of New York were going on, a gentleman from Boston noticed a large quantity of human bones thrown up by the workmen. Everybody knows the African countenance : the skulls also bore unmistakable marks of the race they belonged to. They were shovelled up with the earth which they had rested in, carted off and emptied into the sea to fill up a chasm, and make the foundation of a warehouse.

"On inquiry, the Bostonian learned that these were the bones of colored American soldiers, who fell in the disastrous battles of Long Island, in 1776, and of such as died of the wounds then received. At that day, as at this, spite of the declaration that 'all men are created equal,' the prejudice against the colored man was intensely strong. The black and the white had fought against the same enemy, under the same banner, contending for the same 'unalienable right' to life, liberty, and the pursuit of happiness. The same shot with promiscuous slaughter had mowed down Africans and Americans. But in the grave, they must be divided. On the battle-field, the blacks and whites had mixed their bravery and their blood, but their ashes must not mingle in the bosom of their common mother. The white Saxon, exclusive and haughty even in his burial, must have his place of rest proudly apart from the grave of the African he had once enslaved.

"Now, after seventy-five years have passed by, the bones of these forgotten victims of the Revolution are shovelled up by Irish laborers, carted off, and shot into the sea, as the rubbish of the town. Had they been white men's relics, how would they have been honored with sumptuous burial anew, and the purchased prayers and preaching of Christian divines ! Now, they are the rubbish of the street !

"True, they were the bones of Revolutionary soldiers, — but they were black men; and shall a city that kidnaps its citizens, honor a negro with a grave ? What boots it that he fought for our freedom ; that he bled for our liberty ; that he died for you and me ? Does the 'nigger' deserve a tomb ? Ask the American State—the American Church !

"Three quarters of a century have passed by since the retreat from Long Island. What a change since then ! From
the Washington of that day to the world's Washington of
this, what a change ! In America, what alterations ! What
a change in England ! The Briton has emancipated every
bondman ; slavery no longer burns his soil on either Continent,
the East or West. America has a population of slaves
greater than the people of all England in the reign of Elizabeth. Under the pavement of Broadway, beneath the walls
of the Bazaar, there still lie the bones of the colored martyrs
to American Independence. Dandies of either sex swarm
gaily over the threshold, heedless of the dead African, con-
temptuous of the living. And while these faithful bones
were getting shovelled up and carted to the sea, there was a
great slave-hunt in New York : a man was kidnapped and
carried off to bondage by the citizens, at the instigation of
politicians, and to the sacramental delight of ' divines.'

"Happy are the dead Africans, whom British shot mowed
down ! They did not live to see a man kidnapped in the city
which their blood helped free."

The poor requital for the colored man's valor was forcibly
alluded to by Henry H. Garnet at the anniversary of the
Anti-Slavery Society, in New York city, May, 1840. "It is
with pride," said he, " that I remember, that in the earliest
attempts to establish democracy in this hemisphere, colored
men stood by the side of your fathers, and shared with
them the toils of the Revolution. When Freedom, that had
been chased over half the world, at last thought she had
here found a shelter, and held out her hands for protection,
the tearful eye of the colored man, in many instances, gazed
with pity upon her tattered garments, and ran to her relief.
Many fell in her defence, and the grateful soil received them
affectionately into its bosom. No monumental piles distin-
guish their 'dreamless beds'; scarcely an inch on the page
of history has been appropriated to their memory ; yet truth
will give them a share of the fame that was reaped upon
the fields of Lexington and Bunker Hill ; truth will affirm
that they participated in the immortal honor that adorned
the brow of the illustrious Washington."

GEN. JACKSON'S PROCLAMATION.

"HEADQUARTERS, SEVENTH MILITARY DISTRICT, }
MOBILE, September 21, 1814. }

"*To the Free Colored Inhabitants of Louisiana:*

Through a mistaken policy, you have been heretofore deprived of a participation in the glorious struggle for national rights in which our country is engaged. This no longer shall exist.

As sons of freedom, you are now called upon to defend our most inestimable blessing. As Americans, your country looks with confidence to her adopted children for a valorous support, as a faithful return for the advantages enjoyed under her mild and equitable government. As fathers, husbands, and brothers, you are summoned to rally around the standard of the eagle to defend all which is dear in existence.

Your country, although calling for your exertions, does not wish you to engage in her cause without remunerating you for the services rendered. Your intelligent minds are not to be led away by false representations. Your love of honor would cause you to despise the man who should attempt to deceive you. With the sincerity of a soldier and the language of truth I address you.

To every noble-hearted freeman of color volunteering to serve during the present contest with Great Britain, and no longer, there will be paid the same bounty, in money and lands, now received by the white soldiers of the United States, viz: one hundred and twenty-four dollars in money, and one hundred and sixty acres of land. The non-commissioned officers and privates will also be entitled to the same monthly pay, daily rations and clothes furnished to any American soldier.

On enrolling yourselves in companies, the Major-General commanding will select officers for your government from your white fellow-citizens. Your non-commissioned officers will be appointed from among yourselves.

Due regard will be paid to the feelings of freemen and soldiers. You will not, by being associated with white men in the same corps, be exposed to improper comparison or unjust sarcasm. As a distinct, independent battalion or regiment, pursuing the path of glory, you will, undivided, receive the applause and gratitude of your countrymen.

To assure you of the sincerity of my intentions, and my anxiety to engage your invaluable services to our country, I have communicated my wishes to the Governor of Louisiana, who is fully informed as to the manner of enrolments, and will give you every necessary information on the subject of this address.

ANDREW JACKSON,
Major-General Commanding.

December 18, 1814, General Jackson issued, in the French language, the following address to the colored members of his army : —

"SOLDIERS ! — When, on the banks of the Mobile, I called you to take up arms, inviting you to partake the perils and glory of your white fellow-citizens, I expected much from you ; for I was not ignorant that you possessed qualities most formidable to an invading enemy. I knew with what fortitude you could endure hunger and thirst, and all the fatigues of a campaign. *I knew well how you loved your native country*, and that you, as well as ourselves, had to defend what *man* holds most dear —his parents, wife, children, and property. *You have done more than I expected.* In addition to the previous qualities I before knew you to possess, I found among you a noble enthusiasm, which leads to the performance of great things.

"Soldiers ! the President of the United States shall hear how praiseworthy was your conduct in the hour of danger, and the representatives of the American people will give you the praise your exploits entitle you to. Your General anticipates them in applauding your noble ardor.

"The enemy approaches ; his vessels cover our lakes ; our brave citizens are united, and all contention has ceased among them. Their only dispute is, who shall win the prize of valor, or who the most glory, its noblest reward.

"By order,

"THOMAS BUTLER, *Aid-de-Camp.*"

The New Orleans *Picayune*, in an account of the celebration of the Battle of New Orleans, in that city, in 1851, says: —

"Not the least interesting, although the most novel feature of the procession yesterday, was the presence of ninety of the colored veterans who bore a conspicuous part in the dangers of the day they were now for the first time called to assist in celebrating, and who, by their good conduct in presence of the enemy, deserved and received the approbation of their illustrious commander-in-chief. During the thirty-six years that have passed away since they assisted to repel the invaders from our shores, these faithful men have never before participated in the annual rejoicings for the victory which their valor contributed to gain. Their good deeds have been consecrated only in their memories, or lived but to claim a passing notice on the page of the historian. Yet, who more than they deserve the thanks of the country, and the gratitude of succeeding generations? Who rallied with more alacrity in response to the summons of danger? Who endured more cheerfully the hardships of the camp, or faced with greater courage the perils of the fight? If, in that hazardous hour, when our homes were menaced with the horrors of war, we did not disdain to call upon the colored population to assist in repelling the invading horde, we should not, when the danger is past, refuse to permit them to unite with us in celebrating the glorious event, which they helped to make so memorable an epoch in our history. We were not too exalted to mingle with them in the affray; they were not too humble to join in our rejoicings.

"Such, we think, is the universal opinion of our citizens. We conversed with many yesterday, and, without exception, they expressed approval of the invitation which had been extended to the colored veterans to take part in the ceremonies of the day, and gratification at seeing them in a conspicuous place in the procession.

"The respectability of their appearance, and the modesty of their demeanor, made an impression on every observer, and elicited unqualified approbation. Indeed, though in saying so we do not mean disrespect to any one else, we think that they constituted decidedly the most interesting portion of the pageant, as they certainly attracted the most attention."

The editor, after further remarks upon the procession, and adding of its colored members, " We reflected, that beneath their dark bosoms were sheltered faithful hearts, susceptible of the noblest impulses," thus alludes to the free colored population of New Orleans: —

" As a class, they are peaceable, orderly, and respectable people, and many of them own large amounts of property among us. Their interests, their homes, and their affections are here, and such strong ties are not easily broken by the force of theoretical philanthropy, or imaginative sentimentality. They have been true hitherto, and we will not do them the injustice to doubt a continuance of their fidelity. While they may be certain that insubordination will be promptly punished, deserving actions will always meet with their due reward in the esteem and gratitude of the community."

Yet, if five, even of these veterans, should at any time be seen talking together, they are liable to be arrested for conspiracy, according to the laws of Louisiana!

Hon. Robert C. Winthrop, in his speech in Congress, on the Imprisonment of Colored Seamen, September, 1850, bore this testimony to the gallant conduct of the colored soldiers at New Orleans: —

" I have an impression that, not, indeed, in these piping times of peace, but in the time of war, when quite a boy, I have seen black soldiers enlisted, who did faithful and excellent service. But, however it may have been in the Northern States, I can tell the Senator what happened in the Southern States at this period. I believe that I shall be borne out in saying, that no regiments did better service, at New Orleans, than did the black regiments, which were organized under the direction of General Jackson himself, after a most glorious appeal to the patriotism and honor of the people of color of that region; and which, after they came out of the war, received the thanks of General Jackson, in a proclamation which has been thought worthy of being inscribed on the pages of history."

Chalmette Plains, the scene of the famous Battle of New Orleans, are five miles below that city, on the left bank of the

Mississippi. There is an elaborate engraving of this battle, eighteen by twenty inches, executed by M. Hyacinth Laclotte, the correctness of which was certified to by eleven of the superior officers residing in New Orleans, July 15, 1815, when the drawing was completed.

The report "No. 8," from the American Army, corroborates the following interesting statements, which were furnished to the author of " The Colored Patriots of the American Revolution " by Wm. H. Day, Esq., of Cleveland: —

" From an authenticated chart, belonging to a soldier friend, I find that, in the Battle of New Orleans, Major-General Andrew Jackson, Commander-in-Chief, and his staff, were just at the right of the advancing left column of the British, and that very near him were stationed the colored soldiers. He is numbered 6, and the position of the colored soldiers, 8. The chart explanation of No. 8 reads thus: —
' 8. Captains Dominique and Bluche, two 24 pounders; Major Lacoste's battalion, formed of the men of color of New Orleans, and Major Daquin's battalion, formed of the men of color of St. Domingo, under Major Savary, second in command.'

" They occupied no mean place, and did no mean service.

" From other documents in my possession, I am able to state the number of the 'battalion of St. Domingo men of color' to have been one hundred and fifty; and of 'Major Lacoste's battalion of Louisiana men of color,' two hundred and eighty.

" Thus were over four hundred ' men of color ' in that battle. When it is remembered that the whole number of soldiers claimed by Americans to have been in that battle reached only 3,600, it will be seen that the 'men of color' were present in much larger proportion than their numbers in the country warranted.

" Neither was there colorphobia then. Major Planche's battalion of uniformed volunteer companies, and Major Lacoste's 'men of color,' wrought together; so, also, did Major Daquin's 'men of color,' and the 44th, under Captain Baker.

" Great Britain had her colored soldiers in that battle; the United States had hers. Great Britain's became freemen and citizens : those of the United States continued only half-free and slaves."

During the war of 1812, Capt. Perry, writing to Commodore Chauncy, the senior officer, said—"The men that came by Mr. Champlin are a motley set—blacks, soldiers, and boys. *I am, however, pleased to see any thing in the shape of a man.*" The following letter was sent by Commodore Chauncy in reply:—

"ON BOARD THE PIKE, OFF BURLINGTON BAY,)
July 13th. }

"SIR,—I have been duly honored with your letters of the 23d and 26th ultimo, and notice your anxiety for men and officers. I am equally anxious to furnish you, and no time shall be lost in sending officers and men to you, as soon as the public service will allow me to send them from this lake. I regret that you are not pleased with the men sent you by Messrs. Champlin and Forrest; for, to my knowledge, a part of them are not surpassed by any seamen we have in the fleets; and I have yet to learn that the color of the skin, or the cut and trimmings of the coat, can affect a man's qualifications or usefulness. *I have nearly fifty blacks on board this ship, and many of them are among my best men;* and those people you call soldiers have been to sea from two to seventeen years, and I presume that you will find them as good and useful as any men on board of your vessel; at least, if I can judge by comparison, for those which we have on board this ship are attentive and obedient, and, as far as I can judge, many of them excellent seamen; at any rate, the men sent to Lake Erie have been selected with a view of sending a fair proportion of petty officers and seamen, and I presume, upon examination, it will be found they are equal to those upon this lake."

During the Dorr excitement, the colored population of Rhode Island received high encomiums from the papers of the State for their conduct. The New York *Courier and Enquirer* said:—"The colored people of Rhode Island deserve the good opinion and kind feeling of every citizen of the State, for their conduct during the recent troublous times in Providence. They promptly volunteered their services for any duty to which they might be useful in maintaining law and order. Upwards of a hundred organized themselves for the purpose of acting as a city guard for the protection of the city, and to extinguish fires, in case of their occurrence, while the citizens were absent on military duty. The fathers of these people were distinguished for their patriotism and bravery in the war of the Revolution, and the Rhode Island colored regiment fought, on one occasion, until half their number were slain. There was not a regiment in the service which did more soldierly duty, or showed itself more devotedly patriotic."

EMPLOYMENT OF NEGROES

IN THE

AMERICAN ARMY OF THE REVOLUTION.

BY

GEORGE H. MOORE,

LIBRARIAN OF THE NEW-YORK HISTORICAL SOCIETY.

NEW YORK:

CHARLES T. EVANS, 532 BROADWAY.

1862.

HISTORICAL NOTES

ON THE EMPLOYMENT OF NEGROES IN THE AMERICAN ARMY OF THE REVOLUTION.

THE employment of negroes became a subject of importance at an early stage of the American War of Independence. The British naturally regarded slavery as an element of weakness in the condition of the colonies, in which the slaves were numerous, and laid their plans to gain the blacks, and induce them to take up arms against their masters, by promising them their liberty, on this condition. One of the earliest and most powerful American writers against Slavery (the famous Dr. HOPKINS) wrote thus in 1776:

"God is so ordering it in his providence, that it seems absolutely necessary something should speedily be done with respect to the slaves among us, in order to our safety, and to prevent their turning against us in our present struggle, in order to get their liberty. Our oppressors have planned to gain the blacks, and induce them to take up arms against us, by promising them liberty on this condition; and this plan they are prosecuting to the utmost of their power, by which means they have persuaded numbers to join them. And should we attempt to restrain them by force and severity, keeping a strict guard over them, and punishing them severely, who shall be detected in attempting to join our opposers; this will only be making bad worse, and serve to render our inconsistence, oppression, and cruelty, more criminal, perspicuous, and shocking, and bring down the righteous vengeance of heaven on our heads. The only way pointed out to prevent this threatening evil, is to set the blacks at liberty ourselves, by some public acts and laws; and then give them proper encouragement to labour, or take arms in the defence of the American cause, as they shall choose. This would at once be doing them some degree of justice, and defeating our enemies in the scheme they are prosecuting."

These were the views of a philanthropic divine, who urged them upon the Continental Congress and the owners of slaves throughout the Colonies with singular power, showing it to be at once their duty and their interest to adopt the policy of Emancipation.

Such, however, were not the ruling ideas in administration of any of the Colonies—not even in Massachusetts, although the subject was prominent at an early day. In October, 1774, a formal suggestion was made in their first Provincial Congress of "the propriety, that while we are attempting to free ourselves from our present embarrassments, and preserve ourselves from slavery, that we also take into consideration the state and circumstances of the negro slaves in this province." A motion for a committee to take the subject into consideration, produced some debate, when "the question was put, whether the matter now subside, and it passed in the affirmative."

But while the general question of emancipation was thus allowed to " subside," the exigencies of the contest again and again brought up the practical one of em-

ployment for negroes, whether bond or free; and still
Massachusetts continued to adhere to the conservative
policy.

In May, 1775, the Committee of Safety (Hancock
and Warren's committee)* came to a formal resolution,
which is certainly one of the most significant documents
of the period.

"*Resolved*, That it is the opinion of this Committee, as the contest now between Great Britain and the Colonies respects the
liberties and privileges of the latter, which the Colonies are determined to maintain, that the admission of any persons, as soldiers,
into the army now raising, but only such as are freemen, will be
inconsistent with the principles that are to be supported, and reflect
dishonor on this Colony, and that no slaves be admitted into this
army upon any consideration whatever."

This resolution being communicated to the Provincial Congress (June 6, 1775) was read, and ordered to
lie on the table for further consideration. It was probably allowed to "subside," like the former proposition.

Washington took command of the army around
Boston on the 3d July, 1775.

The instructions for the recruiting officers of the
several regiments of the Massachusetts Bay Forces, 10th
July, 1775, from his head-quarters at Cambridge, prohibited the enlistment of any "negro." It may also be
noticed that they were forbidden to enlist "any Person
who is not an American born, unless such Person has a
Wife and Family and is a settled Resident in this
Country."

---

* It may be gratifying to persons in similar official positions at this
day to know that a citizen of Massachusetts was called to the bar of the
Provincial Congress, and "admonished" for having made use of the following expression, viz.: "By God, if this province is to be governed in
this manner, it is time for us to look out; and 'tis all owing to the Committee of Safety, a pack of sappy-head-fellows. I know three of them
myself."

Notwithstanding all this, the fact is notorious, as Bancroft says, that "the roll of the army at Cambridge had from its first formation borne the names of men of color." "Free negroes stood in the ranks by the side of white men. In the beginning of the war they had entered the provincial army: the first general order which was issued by Ward, had required a return, among other things, of the 'complexion' of the soldiers; and black men, like others, were retained in the service after the troops were adopted by the continent."

On the 26th Sept., 1775, a debate occurred in the Continental Congress, upon the draft of a letter to the Commander in-Chief, reported by Lynch, Lee, and Adams, to whom several of Washington's previous letters had been referred, and E. Rutledge, of South Carolina, moved that the General should be instructed to discharge all the negroes, as well slaves as freemen, in his army. He was strongly supported by many of the Southern delegates, but so powerfully opposed that he lost the point. Again,

"At a council of war, held at head-quarters, October 8th, 1775, present: His Excellency, General Washington; Major-Generals Ward, Lee, and Putnam; Brigadier Generals Thomas, Spencer, Heath, Sullivan, Greene, and Gates—the question was proposed:

"'Whether it will be advisable to enlist any negroes in the new army? or whether there be a distinction between such as are slaves and those who are free?'

"It was agreed unanimously to reject all slaves; and, by a great majority, to reject negroes altogether."

Soon after this, a Committee of Conference, consisting of Dr. Franklin, Benj. Harrison, and Thomas Lynch, met at Cambridge (Oct. 18, 1775), with the Deputy-Governors of Connecticut and Rhode Island, and the Committee of the Council of Massachusetts Bay, to confer with General Washington, and devise a method for renovating the army. On the 23d October, the negro question was presented and disposed of as follows:

"Ought not negroes to be excluded from the new enlistment, especially such as are slaves? all were thought improper by the council of officers."

"*Agreed* that they be rejected altogether."

In general orders, November 12, 1775, Washington says:

"Neither negroes, boys unable to bear arms, nor old men unfit to endure the fatigues of the campaign, are to be enlisted."

, General Washington, however, in the last days of the year, upon representations to him that the free negroes who had served in his army, were very much dissatisfied at being discarded, and fearing that they might seek employment in the ministerial army,* took the responsibility to depart from the resolution respecting them, and gave license for their being enlisted.

In general orders, December 30, he says:

"As the General is informed that numbers of free negroes are desirous of enlisting, he gives leave to the recruiting officers to entertain them, and promises to lay the matter before the Congress, who, he doubts not, will approve of it."

Washington communicated his action to Congress, adding, "If this is disapproved of by Congress, I will put a stop to it."

His letter was referred to a committee of three (Mr. Wythe, Mr. Adams, and Mr. Wilson) on the 15th January, 1776, and upon their report on the following day, the Congress determined—

---

* Washington's apprehensions were grounded somewhat on the operations of Lord Dunmore, whose proclamation had been issued declaring "all indented servants, negroes, or others (appertaining to rebels) free," and calling on them to join his Majesty's troops. It was the opinion of the Commander-in-Chief that, if Dunmore was not crushed before Spring, he would become the most formidable enemy America had; "his strength will increase as a snowball by rolling, and faster, if some expedient cannot be hit upon to convince the slaves and servants of the impotency of his designs."

" That the free negroes who have served faithfully in the army at Cambridge may be re-enlisted therein, but no others."

This limited toleration seems to have exhausted the power in direct action of the United States on the subject of black levies in the army of the Revolution ; but it is by no means to be regarded as a final settlement of the question. Their subsequent action was by recommendation to the States, with a most conservative caution not to infringe upon State rights.

Early in 1779, a proposal was made which promised the best results, had it been fairly put in operation. The following letter from Alexander Hamilton to the President of Congress, written from head-quarters, embodies the views which may be presumed to have prevailed there :

"HAMILTON TO JAY

" HEAD-QUARTERS, *March* 14, 1779.

" DEAR SIR : Colonel Laurens, who will have the honor of delivering you this letter, is on his way to South Carolina, on a project which I think, in the present situation of affairs there, is a very good one, and deserves every kind of support and encouragement. This is, to raise two, three, or four battalions of negroes, with the assistance of the government of that State, by contributions from the owners, in proportion to the number they possess. If you should think proper to enter upon the subject with him, he will give you a detail of his plan. He wishes to have it recommended by Congress to the State ; and, as an inducement, that they would engage to take their battalions into Continental pay.

" It appears to me, that an expedient of this kind, in the present state of Southern affairs, is the most rational that can be adopted, and promises very important advantages. Indeed, I hardly see how a sufficient force can be collected in that quarter without it : and the enemy's operations there are growing infinitely serious and formidable. I have not the least doubt, that the negroes will make very excellent soldiers with proper management : and I will venture to pronounce, that they cannot be put in better hands than those of Mr. Laurens. He has all the zeal, intelligence, enterprise, and every other qualification, requisite to succeed in such an undertaking. It is a maxim with some great military judges, that, with sensible officers, soldiers can hardly be too stupid ; and, on this principle, it is thought that the Russians would make the best soldiers in the world, if they were under other officers than their own. The King of Prussia is among the number who maintain this doctrine, and has a very emphatic saying on the occasion, which I do not exactly recollect. I mention this because I have frequently heard it objected to the scheme of embodying negroes, that they are too stupid to make soldiers. This is so far from appearing to me a valid objection, that I think their want of cultivation (for their natural faculties are as good as ours), joined to that habit of subordination which they acquire from a life of servitude, will enable them sooner to become soldiers than our white inhabitants. Let officers be men of sense and sentiment, and the nearer the soldiers approach to machines, perhaps the better.

" I foresee that this project will have to combat much opposition from prejudice and self-interest. The contempt we have been taught to entertain for the blacks, makes us fancy many things that are founded neither in reason nor experience; and an unwillingness to part with property of so valuable a kind, will furnish a thousand arguments to show the impracticability, or pernicious tendency, of a scheme which requires such sacrifices. But it should be considered, that if we do not make use of them in this way, the enemy probably will; and that the best way to counteract the temptations they will hold out, will be to offer them ourselves. An essential part of the plan is, to give them their freedom with their swords. This will secure their fidelity, animate their courage, and, I believe, will have a good influence upon those who remain, by opening a door to their emancipation.

" This circumstance, I confess, has no small weight in inducing me to wish the success of the project ; for the dictates of humanity and true policy equally interest me in favor of this unfortunate class of men.

" While I am on the subject of Southern affairs, you will excuse the liberty I take in saying, that I do not think measures sufficiently vigorous are pursuing for our defence in that quarter. Except the few regular troops of South Carolina, we seem to be relying wholly on the militia of that and two neighboring States. These will soon grow impatient of service, and leave our affairs in a miserable situation. No considerable force can be uniformly kept up by militia, to say nothing of the many obvious and well-known inconveniences that attend this kind of troops. I would beg leave to suggest, sir, that no time ought to be lost in making a draught of militia to serve a twelve-month, from the States of North and South Carolina and Virginia. But South Carolina, being very weak in her population of whites, may be excused from the draught, on condition of furnishing the black battalions. The two others may furnish about three thousand five hundred men, and be exempted, on that account, from sending any succors to this army. The States to the northward of Virginia, will be fully able to give competent supplies to the army here ; and it will require all the force and exertions of the three States I have mentioned, to withstand the storm which has arisen, and is increasing in the South.

"The troops draughted, must be thrown into battalions, and officered in the best possible manner. The best supernumerary officers may be made use of as far as they will go. If arms are wanted for their troops, and no better way of supplying them is to be found, we should endeavor to levy a contribution of arms upon the militia at large. Extraordinary exigencies demand extraordinary means. I fear this Southern business will become a very *grave* one.

" With the truest respect and esteem,

" I am, sir, your most obedient servant,

ALEX. HAMILTON.

" His Excellency, JOHN JAY,
    President of Congress."

This project of Laurens was most timely. The Southern States were threatened by the enemy, and the circumstances of the army would not admit of the detaching any force for their defence.

The continental battalions of South Carolina and Georgia were far from being adequate to the work.

Three battalions of North Carolina continental troops were at that time on the Southern service; but they were composed of drafts from the militia for nine months only—and the term of service of a great part of them, would expire before the end of the campaign. All the other force then employed for the defence of these States, consisted of militia, who could not justly be relied on for continued exertions and a protracted war.

These views were illustrated and enforced in Congress by a committee, who evidently favored the views of Laurens, sustained as they were by the accredited representatives of his native State, and her government. On the 29th of March, 1779, a committee of Congress, who had been appointed to take into consideration the circumstances of the Southern States, and the ways and means for safety and defence, made their report. South Carolina had made a serious representation of her exposed condition in consequence of the great number of her slaves. She was unable to make any effectual efforts with militia, by reason of the great proportion of citizens necessary to remain at home to prevent insurrections among the negroes, and their desertion to the enemy, who were assiduous in their endeavors to excite both revolt and desertion. Under these circumstances, the delegates from that State, and a special envoy from the Governor suggested "that a force might be raised in the said State from among the negroes, which would not only be formidable to the enemy, from their numbers, *and the discipline of which they would very readily admit*, but would also lessen the dangers from revolts and desertions, by detaching the most vigorous and enterprising from among the negroes. That, as this measure may involve inconveniences peculiarly affecting the State of South Carolina and Georgia, the committee are of opinion that the same should be submitted to the governing powers of the said States; and if the said powers shall judge it expedient to raise such a force, that the United States ought to defray the expense thereof: Whereupon,

" *Resolved*, That it be recommended to the States of South Carolina and Georgia, if they shall think the same expedient, to take measures immediately for raising three thousand able-bodied negroes.

" That the said negroes be formed into separate corps, as battalions, according to the arrangements adopted for the main army, to be commanded by white commissioned and non-commissioned officers.

"That the commissioned officers be appointed by the said States.

"That the non-commissioned officers may, if the said States respectively shall think proper, be taken from among the non-commissioned officers and soldiers of the continental battalions of the said States respectively.

"That the governors of the said States, together with the commanding officer of the Southern army, be empowered to incorporate the several continental battalions of their States with each other respectively, agreeably to the arrangement of the army, as established by the resolutions of May 27, 1778 ; and to appoint such of the supernumerary officers to command the said negroes, as shall choose to go into that service.

"*Resolved,* That Congress will make provision for paying the proprietors of such negroes as shall be enlisted for the service of the United States during the war, a full compensation for the property, at a rate not exceeding one thousand dollars for each active, able-bodied negro man of standard size, not exceeding thirty-five years of age, who shall be so enlisted and pass muster.

"That no pay or bounty be allowed to the said negroes; but that they be clothed and subsisted at the expense of the United States.

"That every negro, who shall well and faithfully serve as a soldier to the end of the present war, and shall then return his arms, be emancipated, and receive the sum of fifty dollars."

Such was the project and such its origin. Full of zeal and enthusiasm in his design, which was the public good, Laurens himself proposed to bear a part in this business, by taking the command of a battalion, and on the same day on which the resolutions were adopted, was appointed by Congress a Lieutenant-Colonel. The resolution is significant.

"Whereas John Laurens, Esq., who has heretofore acted as aide-de-camp to the commander-in-chief, is desirous of repairing to South Carolina, with a design to assist in defence of the Southern States :

"*Resolved,* That a commission of lieutenant-colonel be granted to the said John Laurens, Esq."

He proceeded at once to Charleston to urge upon the authorities of South Carolina the adoption of the proposed plan. A letter from him at this date says: "It appears to me that I should be inexcusable in the light of a citizen, if I did not continue my utmost efforts for carrying the plan of the black levies into execution, while there remains the smallest hope of success. ... The House of Representatives ... will be convened in a few days. I intend to qualify, and make a final effort. Oh that I were a Demosthenes! The Athenians never deserved a more bitter exprobration than our countrymen."

Major-general Greene entertained the same opinions with reference to the black levies, and very emphatically said that he had not the least doubt that the blacks would make good soldiers.

But the project encountered at once that strong, deep-seated feeling, nurtured from earliest infancy among that people, which was ready to decide, with instinctive promptness, against "a measure of so threatening an aspect, and so offensive to that republican (?) pride, which disdains to commit the defence of the country to servile bands, or share with a color, to which the idea of inferiority is inseparably connected, the profession of arms, and that approximation of condition which must exist between the regular soldier and the militia man."

These words are those of the Southern historian who tells us how South Carolina and Georgia were "startled" by this proposal of one of the most gifted of their children.

The Legislature, under the influence of such sentiments, thought the experiment a dangerous one, and the plan was not adopted. Laurens renewed his efforts at a later period of the war, and urged the matter very strenuousiy both to the privy council and legislative body. His own account of his second failure is the best that can be given:

"I was outvoted, having only reason on my side, and being opposed by a triple-headed monster, that shed the baneful influence of avarice, prejudice, and pusillanimity in all our assemblies. It was some consolation to me, however, to find that philosophy and truth had made some little progress since my last effort, as I obtained twice as many suffrages as before."

Washington comforted Laurens with the confession that he was not at all astonished by the failure of the plan, adding:

"That spirit of freedom, which at the commencement of this contest would have gladly sacrificed everything to the attainment of its object, has long since subsided, and every selfish passion has taken its place. It is not the public, but private interest, which influences the generality of mankind, nor can the Americans any longer boast an exception. Under these circumstances it would rather have been surprising if you had succeeded."

In the beginning of the war, the Georgia delegates gave to John Adams, as recorded in his diary at the time, "a melancholy account of the state of Georgia and South Carolina. They said if one thousand regular troops should land in Georgia, and their commander be provided with arms and clothes enough, and proclaim freedom to all the negroes who would join his camp, twenty thousand negroes would join it from the two Provinces in a fortnight. The negroes have a wonderful art of communicating intelligence among themselves; it will run several hundreds of miles in a week or fortnight. They said their only security was this; that all the King's friends, and tools of Government, have large plantations, and property in negroes, so that the slaves of the Tories would be lost, as well as those of the Whigs."

Ramsay, the historian of South Carolina, estimates the loss of negroes during the war by thousands; and states: "It has been computed by good judges that, between the years 1775 and 1783, the State of South Carolina lost twenty-five thousand negroes." This was a fifth part of all the slaves in the State at the beginning of the war, and equal to more than half the entire white population.

In Georgia the loss was greater in proportion, the best authority estimating it at from three-fourths to seven-eighths of all in the State. The British there organized and made use of the negroes. At the siege of Augusta, in 1781, Fort Cornwallis "was garrisoned by four hundred men, in addition to two hundred negroes."

As late as 1786, a corps of runaway negroes, the leaders of which, having been trained to arms by the British during the siege of Savannah, still called themselves the "King of England's soldiers," continued to harass and alarm the people on both sides the Savannah river by their own depredations and the fear that their countenance might lead to a general and bloody insurrection of the slaves in that vicinity. The historian of the State of Georgia, who records their final suppression, speaks of them as "one of the most dangerous and best disciplined bands of marauders which ever infested its borders."

Notwithstanding all his previous discouragements, Laurens, in 1782, took new measures in Georgia on the subject of the black levies, and, as he himself expressed it, "with all the tenacity of a man making a last effort on so interesting an occasion."

But all was of no avail. Though the wisdom of the statesman, the gallantry of the soldier, and the self-devotion of the patriot, which formed the character of John Laurens, were never more conspicuous than in his efforts on this occasion, South Carolina was almost as little able to appreciate them then as she would be to-day. Always hostile to free government, the majority of her population were steeped in toryism, and so wedded to their system then as to refuse to make use of the most certain means of defence against their own oppressors. Grand and glorious names live in the pages of her revolutionary history, but the sentiments and opinions which are their most lasting claims to honor, were then unheeded, and have long since ceased to find an echo in the hearts of their degenerate children.

There can be no doubt that negroes, bond and free, were in the ranks of the American army during the entire period of the war, or that they continued to be enlisted or enrolled in most of the States, especially as the pressure for recruits increased in the later years of the struggle.

Graydon, whose Memoirs are so familiar to the students of our revolutionary history, in his famous description of the army at New York in 1776, makes a favorable exception of Glover's regiment from Marblehead, Mass., among the "miserably constituted bands from New England." "But," he adds, "even in this regiment there were a number of negroes, which, to persons unaccustomed to such associations, had a disagreeable, degrading effect."

It is to be hoped that the researches of our historical scholars will develop more accurate information as to this class of our revolutionary patriots. At present, a deficiency must be noted in this respect. The returns of their numbers, it is to be presumed, were rarely made separately, as they appear to have been scattered through the entire forces; or, if made, have almost entirely escaped notice.

The following return is one of the most interesting memorials of the negro service in the American army of the Revolution, and may be relied on as authentic, as it was official.

RETURN OF NEGROES IN THE ARMY, 24th Aug., 1778.

BRIGADES.	Present.	Sick absent.	On command	Total.
North Carolina.......	42	10	6	58
Woodford	36	3	1	40
Muhlenburg	64	26	8	98
Smallwood	20	3	1	24
2d Maryland.........	43	15	2	60
Wayne..............	2	..	..	2
2d Pennsylvania......	[33]	[1]	[1]	[35]
Clinton.............	33	2	4	39
Parsons.............	117	12	19	148
Huntington..........	56	2	4	62
Nixon	26	..	1	27
Patterson	64	13	12	89
Late Learned........	34	4	8	46
Poor...............	16	7	4	27
Total............	586	98	71	755

ALEX. SCAMMELL,
Adj.-Gen.

This return embraces the negroes with the main army, under General Washington's immediate command, two months after the battle of Monmouth.

Similar returns from the other armies in other departments would doubtless show a larger proportion in many brigades. The black regiment of Rhode Island slaves is not included in the above return, although it

2

had been already organized. Its history is as remarkable as any part of the subject under consideration.

Early in 1778 it was proposed by General Varnum to Washington that the two Rhode Island battalions in camp at Valley Forge should be united, and that the officers of one, Col. Greene, Lieut.-Col. Olney, and Major Ward, with their subalterns, be sent to Rhode Island to enlist a battalion of negroes for the continental service. The plan was approved, and the officers were sent home for that purpose.

The Rhode Island Assembly accordingly resolved to raise a regiment of slaves, who were to be freed upon their enlistment, and their owners to be paid by the State according to the valuation of a committee (of five, one from each county)—one hundred and twenty pounds being the highest price for the most valuable slave. Six deputies protested against this act, on the ground that there were not enough slaves to make an effective regiment; that the measure would be disapproved abroad; that the expense would be greater, and the owners be dissatisfied with the indemnity offered by the State.

The preamble of the act recites the fact that "history affords us frequent precedents of the wisest, freest, and bravest nations having liberated their slaves and enlisted them as soldiers to fight in defence of their country."

Gov. Cooke, in reporting the result to Washington, said: "Liberty is given to every effective slave to enter into the service during the war; and upon his passing muster he is absolutely made free, and entitled to all the wages, bounties, and encouragements given by Congress to any soldier enlisting into their service. . . . . The number of slaves is not great but it is generally thought that three hundred and upwards will be enlisted."

His expectations were not disappointed; and these slaves who were to win their own freedom in fighting for American Independence took the field in force. Before the end of the year, these men were tried and not found wanting. In the battle of Rhode Island, Aug. 29, 1778, said by Lafayette to have been "the best fought action of the whole war," this newly raised black regiment, under Col. Greene, distinguished itself by deeds of desperate valor, repelling three times the fierce assaults of an overwhelming force of Hessian troops. And so they continued to discharge their duty with zeal and fidelity—never losing any of their first laurels so gallantly won. It is not improbable that Col. John Laurens witnessed and drew some of his inspiration from the scene of their first trial in the field.

It will be noticed, that in the absence of a formal system under continental authority, black men continued to find their way into the service, under various laws, and sometimes under no law or in defiance of law. Probably every State had its colored representatives among the soldiery—and there are acknowledgments of services expected or rendered among the records of nearly all the States.

In New Hampshire, those blacks who enlisted into the army for three years, were entitled to the same bounty as the whites. This bounty their masters received as the price of their liberty, and then delivered up their bills of sale, and gave them a certificate of manumission. Most of the slaves in New Hampshire were emancipated by their owners, with the exception of such as had grown old in service, and refused to accept their freedom, remaining with their masters, or as pensioners on the families of their descendants.

In Massachusetts, whose earlier action has been noted, a committee of the Legislature, in 1778, reported in favor of raising a regiment of "negroes, mulattoes, or Indians"—in which one sergeant in each company, and all the higher officers were to be white men.

Connecticut, too, is said to have resorted to the expedient of forming a corps of colored soldiers when the difficulties of recruiting became pressing, and the late General Humphreys, who was attached to the military family of the commander-in-chief, like Laurens, accepted the command of a company of these men, who are said to have "conducted themselves with fidelity and efficiency throughout the war."

In New York, where the system of domestic slavery was as firmly and rigorously established as in any part of the country, under the Colonial laws—certainly with more severity than in either Massachusetts or Connecticut—the first act that went to relax the system was the act of 1781, which gave freedom to all slaves who should serve in the army for the term of three years, or until regularly discharged. The enlistment was to be with the consent of the owner, who received the land bounty, and was discharged from any future maintenance of the slave.

It is a singular contrast that, in New Jersey, the enlistment of slaves was prohibited in the same year, 1781.

In 1780, an act was passed in Maryland to procure one thousand men, to serve three years. The property in the State was divided into classes of £16,000, each of which was, within twenty days, to furnish one recruit, who might be either a freeman or a slave. In 1781, the Legislature resolved to raise, immediately, seven hundred and fifty negroes, to be incorporated with the other troops.

Among the inducements offered to recruits in the

Southern States, "a healthy sound negro, between the ages of ten and thirty years, or sixty pounds in gold or silver, at the option of the soldier in lieu thereof," as well as the land bounty, were given (in Virginia) to soldiers already enlisted, or who should enlist and serve to the end of the war.

South Carolina gave a similar bounty,—" one sound negro between the age of ten years and forty," " for each and every year's service," to soldiers enlisted for three years or during the war.

The idea that the negroes might be put to a better use did not escape all the statesmen of Virginia. James Madison, at that time a member of the Continental Congress, expressing his satisfaction with the determination of the Legislature of that State to recruit their line of the army for the war, refers to the " negro bounty" as follows:

"Without deciding on the expediency of the mode under their consideration, would it not be as well to liberate and make soldiers at once of the blacks themselves, as to make them instruments for enlisting white soldiers? It would certainly be more consonant to the principles of liberty, which ought never to be lost sight of in a contest for liberty; and with white officers and a majority of white soldiers, no imaginable danger could be feared from themselves, as there certainly could be none from the effect of the example on those who should remain in bondage; experience having shown that a freedman immediately loses all attachment and sympathy with his former fellow-slaves."

In Virginia, an act was passed in 1777, that no negro should be enlisted without a certificate of freedom, the preamble to which declares that slaves had deserted their masters, and under pretence of being freemen had enlisted as soldiers.

In the "Old Dominion," too, many persons during the course of the war caused their slaves to enlist, having tendered them to the recruiting officers as substitutes for free persons, whose lot or duty it was to serve in the army, at the same time representing that these slaves were freemen. On the expiration of the term of enlistment, the former owners attempted to force them to return to a state of servitude, with equal disregard of the principles of justice and their own solemn promise.

The infamy of such proceedings aroused a just indignation, and led to an Act of Emancipation of all slaves who had been thus enlisted and served their term faithfully. The act acknowledged that such persons having "contributed towards the establishment of American liberty and independence, should enjoy the blessings of freedom as a reward for their toils and labors;" and authorized them to sue *in forma pauperis* and to recover damages, if detained in slavery.

Even in South Carolina, an Act was passed in 1783, enfranchising the wife and child of a negro slave, who had been employed by Governor Rutledge as a spy during the war. The diligence and fidelity which he displayed in executing the commissions with which he was intrusted, and the important information which he obtained from within the enemy's lines, frequently at the risk of his life, are duly commemorated in the act; and the emancipation of his wife and child was his "just and reasonable" reward. It does not appear whether the slave himself ever became a freeman.

Another document will serve to illustrate the subject still further—*fas est ab hoste doceri*. Lord Dunmore's offers, in 1775, have already been alluded to, and are familiar to most readers; those of Sir Henry Clinton in 1779, which follow, have hitherto attracted less attention.

" *By his Excellency, Sir* HENRY CLINTON, *K.B., General, and Commander-in-Chief of all His Majesty's Forces within the Colonies lying on the Atlantic Ocean, from Nova Scotia to West Florida, inclusive, &c., &c., &c.:*

" PROCLAMATION.

" WHEREAS, The Enemy have adopted a practice of enrolling NEGROES among their troops: I do hereby give Notice, that all NEGROES taken in Arms, or upon any military Duty, shall be purchased for [*the public service at*] a stated price ; the Money to be paid to the Captors.

" But I do most strictly forbid any Person to sell or claim Right over any NEGROE, the Property of a Rebel, who may take refuge with any part of this Army : And I do promise to every NEGROE who shall desert the Rebel Standard full Security to follow within these Lines any occupation which he shall think proper.

" Given under my Hand, at Head-Quarters,
PHILIPSBURGH, the 30th day of June,
1779.

" H. CLINTON.

" By his Excellency's Comman ,
    JOHN SMITH, Secretary."

When this proclamation was first issued, the words enclosed within brackets were not in it. They were added in the publication two months later—with a statement that the omission was a mistake of the printers.

This proclamation does not appear to have elicited any official notice by the American authorities, but there is a spirited article on the subject, by an " American Soldier," in one of the newspapers of the day, in which he says:

" Justice, honor and freedom are concerned for all men, of whatever nation or kindred, who are in the service of the United States, and fight under the banner of freedom ; therefore I have long expected some notice from authority would have been taken of that insulting and villanous proclamation. Justice demands retalia-

tion for every man in the service of these States, who
may be injured by the ruffian tyrant or any of his slaves;
and his slave Sir Harry ought to be told what retalia-
tion he is to expect from the insulted majesty of our
nation in this instance."

———

These notes might be extended—but enough has
been presented to illustrate the importance of the subject, and in part to show how it was treated in the ancient "times of trial." It requires little ingenuity to
invent historical parallels—not very profound research
to find historical precedents—but it is the highest wisdom to know how to apply the lessons of the Past. As
Mr. Ruffhead said of the ancient statutes, " though
they do not *govern*, they have been found proper to
guide."

New York, *July*, 1862.

MISSING PAGES

IN

AMERICAN HISTORY

REVEALING THE SERVICES OF NEGROES IN THE EARLY WARS IN THE UNITED STATES OF AMERICA

1641 - 1815

BY

LAURA E. WILKES

TEACHER IN THE PUBLIC SCHOOLS
OF WASHINGTON, D. C.

FOREWORD.

 PATIENT research, extending over a period of six years, has given the author the courage to send out this volume. It has also convinced her that the Negroes of America have done their bit in every war and taken no small part in every military movement made for the salvation of this country from the time of its earliest settlement.

The facts found herein are taken from colonial records, state papers, assembly journals, histories of slavery, and old time histories of the various colonies, and of the republic. The reader can easily verify this statement by using the bibliograpy at the end of the work.

While it is impossible to gather all of the truth concerning this matter it is doubtless true, that much more, than is here chronicled, will be available to the student of this particular department of history, if he shall have leisure and funds to dig deeper into half-forgotten traditions of old towns and villages. That these pages may prove a stimulant for farther research, by others, their writer ardently desires and she earnestly hopes the book will eventually be read collaterally, with the histories of the United States, by every one who can be inspired by its information.

L. E. W.

Missing Pages in American History.

DEFENSE SERVICES OF NEGROES IN COLONIAL WARS.
1641-1755.

It appears that on every hand the white settlers were at first kindly received by the original inhabitants of the Amercian soil. It, however, came about as the Indians realized that their hunting grounds were being turned into tilled fields and that thriving villages and towns were taking the place of their forests, that had afforded them everything needful for their existence, fear, distrust, and hatred became the substitutes for friendly interest. Each new settlement made by the white men showed the red men only too plainly that they who had been the sovereigns of the woodland and the stream were rapidly becoming the subjects of foreign masters. Death, migration, or civilization, little of which latter was offered by the British to the aboriginees, were all, to them, equally objectionable and they fell upon the only feasible plan, that of making war, in the hope of exterminating those who were the cause of their sorrows. Dating from the infancy of the English and the Dutch Colonies there were frequent and very terrible outbreaks on the part of the Indians all up and down the Atlantic Coast. For their protection the colonists were forced to provide defense of no uncertain sort. To this end they enacted laws for the calling, of men to arms, as well as for the training of these men in the carrying of the same. Very early in the history of every colony from New Hampshire to Georgia, Negro slavery existed in one form or another, and in many, if not in all of them, the masters did not hesitate to call upon their bondmen to render assistance in the shouldering of arms, and this call received a willing response.

NEW YORK.

The first slaves were carried into the colony of New Amsterdam by the Dutch West India Company from Spanish possessions in 1626. It happened that in 1641, only a few years later, the Dutch, by law, armed these people with a tomyhawk and a half pike to aid them in fighting murderous Indians. In 1664 the Hollanders put their slaves to work throwing up breastworks to defend the city against the English sent by Charles the Second. The people of this colony did not object, on the whole, to the coming of the English, and in a short time after their advent terms were agreed upon which changed the name of the settlement to New York, and placed it under England's control. The black men had evidently given satisfactory service, for in April, 1699, the Earl of Belmont, writing to the Lords of Trade, said:

"But rather than require more soldiers from England, I should advise the sending for negroes from Guinea, which I understand are bought there and brought hither, all charges whatever being borne, for ten pounds apiece, New York money, and I can clothe and feed them very comfortably for nine pence apiece per day sterling money, which is threepence per day less than I require for soldiers."

In this colony, in the year 1693, Negroes and others not listed were ordered to work on the fortifications whenever they needed repairing, under the captains in whose wards they resided. This enactment went into effect in the time of King William's War and enabled Negroes to aid in bringing that struggle to an end. This war extended from 1689 to 1697. The horrible massacre of Schenectady took place at that time, and Port Royal was captured by the English under Sir William Phipps.

A Border Story.

Long after King William's War and Queen Anne's War, Indian hostilities continued in this colony. Villages were often burned, and traveling, as well as hunting parties, were attacked on the roads. In 1749 two Dutchmen, Duk Van Vost and Daniel Toll, with Ryckert, the Negro slave of the latter, were out looking for some horses that had strayed from a farm about three miles from the west of Schenectady. The Hollanders had gone out with a large body of their countrymen, whom they left in order to more successfully carry on their search. Shortly after they left the main party it was attacked by Indians. This they learned from one of the number who had escaped. Fearing for their lives Van Vost and Toll hid themselves and sent Ryckert on to Schenectady to give the alarm and, if possible, to secure aid for them. This he did, and a small body of militia at his direction left the village and proceeded toward the farm to which the two white men had said they would endeavor to make their way. The faithful Ryckert did not remain in town, as he might have been expected to have done, but instead made his way back to the hiding place of his master, Toll, and together they pushed on to the point where it had been agreed that they should meet the militia. In this they were unsuccessful, for they were overtaken by the Indians and Toll was slain. Ryckert, however, was uninjured, and started again for the town. On his way he met the rescue party, who had been delayed, and he offered to return with them and to show them where his master had fallen. On being given a horse he conducted the men to the place. The Indians meanwhile, unsuspected by the whites, still lingered in the neighborhood, looking for more victims. Indeed, they had prepared a decoy in the belief that some one would come to look for the slain Dutch farmer. They propped the dead man's body in an upright sitting position and with a string tied a live crow to it. The bird, of course, hopped up and down in an effort to get away. This is what the rescuers saw when they came upon the scene and, not knowing the man was dead, nor seeing the string fastened to the crow, they rushed forward to examine what appeared to be a wonderful sight—a bird continuing to hop up and down in one place in front of a man. The red men, who had concealed themselves nearby, had anticipated this and they rushed out and killed many of them. There were seventy men in this band of militia. It is not recorded that Ryckert was slain.

MASSACHUSETTS.

The first Negro slaves landed on the bleak and stormy shores of Massachusetts from Bermuda in 1638. Very shortly after this some of these men were called upon to help fight the Indians; for in 1643, when a list was prepared in Plymouth of men capable of bearing arms, it contained the name of Abraham Pearse and described him as being a blackamore. In 1652 an act was passed in this colony requiring that: "All Negroes and Indians from sixteen to sixty years of age, inhabitants or servants to the English, be listed and hereby enjoined to attend trainings as well as the English." These trainings were held at regular intervals. The only music employed was that of a drum. This law was repealed in 1656, but in 1660 all of the males, regardless of race, were required to attend trainings. This statute was set aside, in its turn, and it was not until the administration of Sir Edmund Andros that it was again decreed that no one above the age of fifteen should remain unenlisted by himself or by his master, Negroes not excepted. This law was probably in effect during King William's War, which began in 1693. In 1707 free Negroes and mulattoes of Massachusetts were required to perform services equivalent to that of the militia, under the command of the officers in charge of the military district in which they lived. Under this enactment they served on the highways. Thirty of these people living in the city of Boston are reported as having served in this capacity, giving two hundred and eighteen days of labor. Queen Anne's War was at its height at this time. It was during this period, 1702-1713, that the English colonists suffered terribly at the hands of the French and their Canadian allies, who, dividing themselves into many bands, came down from Maine and made attacks upon a number of the flourishing villages of Massachusetts. Deerfield was sacked in this conflict.

NORTH CAROLINA.

The Virginia planters, moving southward, carried their slaves into North Carolina before 1658, where a special impetus was added to their importation into that colony in that every master was offered fifty acres of land for each servant* over fifteen years of age who could be armed in time of need. In the words of the ancient law referred to, * * * "They to be armed with a good firelock or matchlock bore, twelve bullets to ten pounds of powder and twenty pounds of bullets with match proportionable." (Guns at this time were fired by applying a match to a touchhole.) Several other laws similar to this were passed in the early days of North Carolina for the defense of her settlements. In 1706 all free men of this colony from sixteen to sixty, unless exempted by law, were required to organize as well as keep themselves supplied with ammunition, and whenever an Indian outbreak occurred, all ablebodied men, slave as well as free, were called upon to render military services.

THE TUSCARORA WAR.

The provinces at this period were for the most part wild, unbroken forests. The settlements were small towns, at the mouths of rivers and on islands along the coast. Away from these places were vast stretches of primeval forest, or great swamps filled with tangled thickets. There were no roads other than the highways from one post to another, and these were lonely and deserted. In this great region, twenty-eight Indian tribes, friendly at first to the whites, began to grow irritable and warlike at their constant encroachments. The red men began hostilities in 1711 near Roanoke,

---

*Slave.

North Carolina. Here in one night thirty-seven settlers were put to death. This was the opening scene of the Tuscarora War. It lasted two years. Most of its battles were fought on the soil of the Old North State. Free men of color, by an act of 1706, saw service in this conflict.

With the assistance of their neighbors from South Carolina and Virginia the whites succeeded in conquering the savages, and the Tuscaroras migrated northward and cast in their lot with their kinsmen, the Five Nations, in the vicinity of the Great Lakes.

SOUTH CAROLINA.

Sir John Yemans carried slaves into South Carolina to work his plantations, on the Ashley River, in 1671. Negroes were at work a few years later on the breastworks of Charleston. An act which employed them, reading as follows: "Be it further enacted: That the said William Rhett (commander for managing fortifications) shall have power and is hereby authorized and empowered to press any Negroes within the aforesaid limits (a specified portion of Charleston) to work at the rate of two royals* and a half per diem, their masters finding the victuals, excepting the said Negroes are tradesmen, and then, if wanted, to be pressed to work, at three royals per diem, their masters finding the victuals; and shall also have power to press white men for overseers, within the precincts aforesaid, at the rate of two shillings sixpence per diem." The part of the city fortified had a front on the Cooper River. The Negroes were furnished tools, carts and horses. They made entrenchments, flankers and parapets.

The very next year, 1704, a law was enacted reading as subjoined, which called upon slaves to render military aid in time of alarm. "Whereas, among the several slaves belonging to this colony there are a great number of them who, by care and discipline may be rendered serviceable towards the defense and preservation of this province, and in case of actual invasion, and in order to make the assistance of our trusty slaves more certain and regular: First. Be it enacted by His Excellency, John P. Granville, Palatine, and the rest of the true and absolute lords of this province, by and with the advice and consent of the rest of the members of the General Assembly now met at Charleston, for the southwest part of this province and by the authority of the same: That within thirty days after the ratification of this act, the several captains or commanders

---

*The writer is unable to ascertain the value of a "royal" in present-day money.

throughout this province do, by virtue of a warrant, under their hands and seals, empower and commission five freeholders, in their respective divisions, to form and complete a list of such Negro, mulatto and Indian slaves as they, or any three of them, shall judge serviceable for the purpose aforesaid, which said commanders, after having finished their said lists, are to warn and summon the said masters and mistresses, or overseers, to whom said slaves belong, to appear before them at a certain date to show cause why their said slave or slaves so chosen should not continue the said list: of which reason the said commanders or any three of them are made competent judges, to allow or disapprove as they, in their discretion, shall see fit; and further, to direct and require the said masters and mistresses, or overseers, of said slaves, on time of alarm or special summons, that they cause their several slaves so enlisted, and armed with a serviceable lance, hatchet or gun, with sufficient ammunition, according to the convenience of the said owners, to appear under the colors of the respective captains in their several divisions throughout this province, there to remain and to be disposed in such manner as said officers or the commander-in-chief shall direct and appoint for the public service. And the said commissioners are hereby directed and required that within ten days after completing said list they do return the same to their respective captains in each division under their hands, and upon their oaths, as a true, fair and impartial list of said slaves, according to the best of their judgment; the oath to be administered by the several captains on the return of said lists. And the said captains are hereby also required, that within ten days after the receipt of said list, they present the same to the Right Honorable, the Governor, and receive such instructions for the management of such slaves as His Honor shall prescribe and think fit, and as may best suit the public safety intended thereby."

Section 3: "If any slaves, enlisted as aforesaid, shall happen to be killed or maimed in actual service by the enemy, then the master or owner of such slave so killed or maimed as aforesaid shall be satisfied for the same by the public at such rate of value as the freeholders of the neighborhood, appointed by the governor, on their oaths shall award; on which award so returned the governor is hereby empowered to order the receiver to pay the same."

The above act was in effect two years. The conduct of the drafted black men was doubtless satisfactory, for at the end of that period they were continued in the service through more laws of the Colonial Lords which declared: Whereas, it is necessary for the safety of this province, in case of actual invasion, to have the assistance of our trusty slaves to serve us against our enemies, and it being reasonable that said slaves should be rewarded for the good services they may do us, and a satisfaction may be made the owners of such slaves, either on their death, freedom or maiming:

Section 1: Be it enacted that His Excellency, John, Lord Granville, Palatine, and the rest of the true and absolute lords and proprietors of the province, by and with the concent of the rest of the members of the General Assembly, now met at Charleston for the southwest part of this province, and by the authority of the same: That, within fifteen days after the ratification of this act the several captains of patrol, captains, lieutenants and ensigns of the companies throughout this province, form and complete a list of such Negro, mulatto and Indian slaves as they or any two of them shall judge serviceable for the purpose aforesaid, not exceeding the number of white men under the command of each respective captain, excepting one man slave who shall be at the choice of his master to attend him, upon alarms, armed with a gun and a hatchet or a cutlass at his own proper cost and charge.

Section 3: Every slave enlisted as aforesaid, upon an alarm, shall repair to the colors of their respective captains in their several divisions throughout this province, and on actual invasion shall be accoutred and armed by the captain of each division out of the public store with a launce (lance) and a hatchet or a gun, with ammunition sufficient, and if as aforesaid, by their respective master, mistress or overseer the same (slave) is lost, or damaged, to be paid and allowed them by the public, and the said officers are further directed and required that within five days after completing the said list they do return the same, under their hands and upon their oaths as true, fair and impartial lists of said slaves according to the best of their judgments. The oath to be administered by the next justice of the peace.

Section 5: If any slave shall, in actual invasion, kill or take one or more of our enemies, and the same shall prove, by any white person, to be done by him, he shall, for his reward, at the charge of the public, have and enjoy his freedom for such, his killing or taking as aforesaid; and the master or owner of such slave shall be paid and satisfied by the public at such rates and prices as three freeholders of the neighborhood, who know the said slave, being nominated and appointed by the Right Honorable the Governor, or governor for the time being, shall award, on their oaths, on which award so returned the governor, or governor for the time being, is hereby empowered to order the public receiver to pay the same accordingly. And if any of the said slaves happen to be killed or taken in actual service of this province by the enemy, or afterward enlisted as aforsaid, shall desert and run over to the enemy in time of an invasion, then the master or owner shall be paid and satisfied for him in such manner and form as before appointed to the owner whose slaves are set free.

Section 6: And be it further enacted, by authority aforesaid: That if any slave in actual service of this province is wounded so that he is disabled for service to his master or owner, then such slave so disabled shall be set free at the charge of the public.

This law also contained an act providing for a fine of the officers who failed to put it into execution, as well as one for to punish the owners of slaves who did not comply with its requirements.

THE YEMASEE WAR.

Two years after the struggle with the Tuscaroras in North Carolina came the Yemasee War, in 1715, which threatened the very life of the colony of South Carolina. The Yemasees were a very powerful tribe of redskins, with large possessions in the neighborhood of Port Royal. They were joined by their neighbors, the Muskogees, the Appalachians, Catawbas, Congarees and Cherokees. Indeed, all of the Indians living between Cape Fear and Florida banded together, determined to destroy the settlement on the Ashley River. Craven was at that time the governor of the colony. He put an embargo on all ships, proclaimed martial law and armed a band of trusty Negroes to co-operate with the whites in their military operations. One of these was the defense of a fortification on Goose Creek. This place was defended by forty black and seventy white men, who had decided to remain there until their last drop of blood was shed. Although there were four hundred men in the ranks of their enemy, the settlers held out until the afternoon. The Indians then made overtures of peace. They were admitted into the stockade and immediately slew its defenders. The war continued three years. Its closing scene is considered the "most bloody battle" in the life of the provinces. This occurred when the redskins, after a season of uncertain events on both of the contending sides, were driven southward from their camps across the Salkihatchi River and a large number of them were slain. Many Negroes fell in this battle. Many slaves who rendered military service at this time were set free. They were not in separate ranks, but marchd side by side with the whites.

RHODE ISLAND.

Slavery was introduced into the Colony of Rhode Island in the year 1647. All men within this colony from the age of sixteen to sixty were in the militia in the year 1708 by law. This meant freemen and bondmen, both black and white. Queen Anne's war was being waged at this time.

VIRGINIA.

The first Negroes who arrived in the Colony of Virginia were nineteen persons, who landed at Jamestown in the year, 1619. Let it be said here, by the way, that had these people been citizens of a civilized country they might have been given the protection received by captives under international law, for they were the victims of piracy, having been taken from Spanish-American dominions on a filibustering trip of the ship that brought them here. The Virginia planters realized this fact, too, for they were treated by them as political slaves only, that is to say, they were placed in the hands of the town officials, for whom they worked, or for the town itself. While Negroes very probably rendered some military assistance in Virginia prior to the year 1636, when they were by law excused from carrying or owning arms, the first recorded act calling them into such service was passed in 1723, when it was ordered that: "Free Negroes, mulattoes and Indians as are capable may be listed and employed as drummers or trumpeters, and upon any invasion, insurrection or rebellion all free Negroes, mulattoes or Indians shall be obliged to attend and march with the militia and do the duty of pioneer, or any such other servile duty as they may be directed to perform." In the same year, a little later, another act armed these men, when it was declared that: "Every free Negro, mulatto or Indian being a housekeeper shall be enlisted in the militia, and may be permitted to keep one gun, powder and shot; * * * and that all Negroes, mulattoes or Indians, bond or free, being at any frontier plantation, shall be permitted to keep and use guns, powder and shot or other weapons, offensive or defensive, having first obtained a license for the same from some justice of the peace of the county wherein such plantations lie." This license could be granted upon the application of their owners or upon that of the Negroes themselves. There were many free Negroes in this settlement at this time. Some had secured their liberty by purchasing it; others through Free Issue laws, meritorious acts, or through manumission by Quakers or other conscientious persons. This latter method of setting people free began as early as 1668. The services of this class (the free Negro) were retained in the army through another act of the General Assembly, passed in 1738; but at that time they were employed only as pioneers, drummers or trumpeters. It is pretty safe to say in the latter capacity they made most of the music to which the colonials marked time in those days. In 1755 this law was renewed and they were also required to attend the military trainings held in the province.

GEORGIA.

Georgia was settled in 1732 by the English under Oglethorpe. What is now Florida was then a Spanish province. The Spaniards wished to hold Georgia also, and a conflict arose between them and the English for its possession. Realizing the attitude of the Spanish, Oglethorpe marched across Georgia in the spring of 1740 with the intention of taking the fortification of Saint Augustine. In this he was disappointed. That stronghold was so well defended that the English failed outright. Its garrison was made up of seven hundred regulars, two troops of horse and four companies of armed Negroes. Many, if not all, of the latter had at various times left the plantations of the settlers of the Carolinas, as well as of Georgia, because of a freer life offered to them by the Spanish government in her province of Florida. In 1742, in order to promote their cause, the Spanish fitted out an expedition in Havana to proceed against Oglethorpe. They landed near his fortifications in June of the same year. In this expedition there was a regiment of Negroes, with officers of the same race, bearing the same rank as Spanish officers and similarly clothed in gold and fine lace. "They also talked with the commander-in-chef, Don Antonio de Rodundo, with equal social equality." This undertaking was not a success and Georgia remained an English province.

NEGROES IN THE FRENCH AND INDIAN WAR.

Until a period very near the Revolutionary War the best fur-producing regions, as well as the best fishing grounds on the American continent, were the property of the French, who also controlled the country's waterways. This state of affairs gave the French several advantages over the English in that the former thereby not only managed the sales of the two staples exported from Northern North America, but also had easy access to the section containing the same. The knowledge of this was most distasteful to England, who had a larger population in the new world than France. She had also better situation for commercial enterprises, both home and foreign, as well as direct relation with the mother country through her settlements on the coast. At this time the English, through Cabot, claimed all of the land north and south fiom New Foundland to Florida, and west to the Pacific Ocean, while the French, on their own explorations, owned that part of the continent adjacent to the St. Lawrence and the Mississippi Rivers. In various parts of these regions the latter erected forts.

Frequent disputes arose over the boundaries of the possessions of the two countries. As early as 1690 conflicts occurred in which both sides were aided by friendly Indians and sometimes by Negroes. The French were more favored by the redskins than the English. This was due to the fact, doubtless, that the former were more tactful in their dealings with the savages because they saw, sooner than the English, the wisdom of holding friendly relations with them. Outbreaks occurred in sections far apart from each other. Between 1690 and 1697 the French had won and lost Arcadia. A little later came trouble in New Hampshire and in Massachusetts. In 1702 all cf New England was involved in the bloody struggle known as Queen Anne's War. In 1711 the English of New Jersey and New York, with their dark-skinned allies, marched against the French in Montreal.

By 1716 the English had opened a road across the Blue Ridge Mountains and had made settlements on the Oswego River by 1721. This made them neighbors of the Five Nations, living in the region about the Great Lakes. The French, fearing the friendliness, which they saw growing between the Indians and the English in this section might result unfavorably to them, planned to break up the latter's strength. To that end they made stronger their own holdings by erecting defenses on Lake Champlain and by inviting the French of New Foundland and Arcadia to leave those settlements and go to Louisburg. Both of these places had formerly been ceded to Great Britain. The English objected to the exodus that resulted and did what they could to prevent it. This was followed by more outbreaks and there was serious trouble in Maine. At this period Negroes of Massachusetts saw defensive service. There was Nero Benson, from Framingham. He was a trumpeter in the company of Capt. Isaac Clark. He entered His Majesty's service August 27, 1723. Black men were called to duty not only on land but also on sea at this time, for record is made of Caeser ———, a Negro, in a list of officers and men on board the transport sloop George. He was registered in March, 1722. About this time both countries began to fill the valley of the Ohio with settlers. The French marked, with leaden plates, their sections at the mouths of the various tributaries of this stream. This brought about bloody border fights, as the fertile lands became more and more populated and filled with French bases for military operations.

The struggle, which ended the dispute for this coveted territory, began in 1753, when the French built forts on the land of the Ohio Company, an English firm holding a grant from the King to regions near the Ohio River. This corporation had been organized to settle the country and to trade in fur with the Indians. A road was opened for their operation from the headwaters of the Potomac River, in Maryland, to the present site of Pittsburgh, Pennsylvania, and some settlements were made along the river banks. In a short time thereafter a dispute arose with the French over one of the boundaries of this point, and George Washington, then not more than twenty-three years of age, was sent by the Governor of Virginia with a protest to the French commander, St. Pierre, stationed at Fort Le Beuf. When Washington returned from what was then a long and perilous journey, he reported that the French not only refused to give up the disputed territory but were making warlike preparations for a struggle to keep it. Realizing that war was inevitable, the English also began to make ready for it. They made an effort to dislodge the French from the property of the Ohio Company in 1754. In this they were unsuccessful.

BRADDOCK'S CAMPAIGN.

Following the failure of the English colonists to take the disputed territory from the French, the mother country took a hand in the matter and early in 1755 sent over Gen. Braddock from England with three thousand picked veterans to take charge of military affairs and to direct an expedition against Fort Duquesne. Braddock reached Hampton Roads in February of the same year, and proceeding up the Potomac River, landed in Alexandria, Virginia,

Here, after a short stay, during which he held many discussions with several of the colonial governors as to the management of the war he was about to wage, he crossed the Potomac River, disembarking at what was then Georgetown, Maryland, and started on a slow and roundabout march to Pennsylvania. Because of the condition of the roads the army traveled only a few men deep and was consequently nearly four miles long. The baggage train was made up of two hundred wagons and nearly twenty-five hundred horses. The commander-in-chief traveled in a stately and very cumbersome coach which he had purchased in Alexandria. Many of the wagoners at this time were Negroes. Among them were Sandy Jenkins, of Fairfax County, Virginia. This man lived to be the great age of one hundred and fifteen, dying in Lancaster, Ohio, in February, 1849. The legislative act through which he was doubtless enlisted has been referred to elsewhere in these pages.

In the ranks led by Braddock were several companies of Independents from South Carolina and New York. Black men were among their number and were with them when a halt was made at Fort Fredericktown, now Frederick, Maryland, on May 13, 1755. There they (black men) helped to clear ground and took part in a parade at two o'clock on the evening of that day. It is evident that Braddock picked up black recruits in several places on his line of march to Fort Duquesne. In Pennsylvania there was Capt. Jack, called "Black Jack" and sometimes "Susquehanna Jack." He was a well-known scout and a fearless Indian hunter of mixed blood, Caucasian and African. This man lived on the Juanita River, and his hatred for Indians was very great because his whole family had been murdered by them. He dressed as they did, and often with a band of followers made war upon them. He offered his services to Braddock gratuitously with those of his men, who were all familiar with the woods, if they might go as free lances in the expedition. Although Jack had already rendered personal service to no small degree as a guide to the general, his offer was not accepted by the strict disciplinarian. Pennsylvania sent another of her darker sons in the person of Billy Brown, of Frankfort, to help in the attack on the French fortification. He was born in Africa and was brought to this country a slave. He was alive in 1826 at the age of ninety. From Buck County in the same state came another Negro, Jack Miner, who went as a recruit in the company of Capt. Walker. There, too, were Abraham Lawrence and Archibald Kelso.

When within eight miles of the fort the English were attacked by the French and Indians. The Irish General, Braddock, had the most pronounced objection to his men's fighting from behind trees, as was the American style, adopted from the savages, and they consequently fell into an ambuscade. Unnecessarily exposing himself to the foe, the leader had four horses shot under him. On the fifth he received a wound that ended his life. As he lay dying on the ground he bequeathed to George Washington, Bishop, a very dignified black man, who is described as being the general's bodyguard. Others of the same race as Bishop at this time with Washington were Gilbert and John Alton.

THE SURRENDER OF FORT DUQUESNE.

In 1756 the British lost much that they had won in the vicinity of the Great Lakes, in the colony of New York, and things were not much better for them the following year. In 1758 three campaigns were planned. One of these was another attack on Fort Duquesne, which at that time was still in the hands of the French. The Virginia regiments of the army were then under the command of Washington. He arrived at Fort Cumberland (Cumberland, Maryland), on July 2nd, and began cutting the road to Raystown, now known as Bedford, Pennsylvania. This finished, he there awaited the approach of the rest of the army, under Gen. Forbes. In August of the same year (1758) thirteen colored men were in camp at this place, eight of whom were with the Royal American Regiment. In September three black men were reported as being connected with the Sixty-seventh Regiment, First Highlanders, in camp at Raystown. All of the points mentioned were not far from Fort Duquesne. Raystown, however, not proving near enough to the coveted point for satisfactory military operation, another post was established at Loyal Hanna (Ligionier) with Col. Bouquet as commander. He had here a force of two thousand men. A list, capulated "Effective Rank and File," reports that thirty-six Negroes were with these men under Col. Washington on October 21, 1758. It was on the 24th of November that these black and white men of arms began their march to assail Fort Duquesne. When in sight of the place they discovered it was on fire. Its magazine had been blown up by the French commander who, knowing the strength of the force proceeding against him, realized that there was nothing for him but defeat.

RAIDS.

During this period many unattached bands of Indians made raids in various parts of the country, often unexpectedly, as allies of the

French, swooping down on the settlements of the English and reaping a bloody harvest. More than one of these outbreaks occurred in the neighborhood of Fort Cumberland, in Western Maryland. On one occasion, to punish the redskins, a band of volunteers under Col. Creasap marched as far as what is now known as Negro Mountain. With them was a black man of gigantic stature, who was killed on the mountain in the fierce fight that followed after they met the Indians. It is this event that immortalizes the name Negro on the ridge near the headwaters of the Potomac, for the high land has been called Negro Mountain ever since.

Northern Campaigns.

In the year 1758 new expeditions were also sent against Crown Point and Ticonderoga, both in the hands of the enemy, in Northern New York. The first of these fortifications was built by the French in 1741. During the conflict the English had made several previous efforts to secure it, always to fail. This time, however, they outnumbered the enemy, whose commander, realizing his inability to hold out against such a force, set the fort afire and then abandoned it. About the same time an advance was made upon Ticonderoga and the English secured it in much the same way. In their ranks on the occasion of both of these attacks were a number of Negroes from the northern colonies, especially Massachusetts. One of these is recorded as Caesar ———, of Westfield, a private under Jedidiah Preeble, and another of the same race, from Hingham, bearing a similar name. Black militiamen were seen also at this period at Fort Williams, a stockade on the road to Oswego, New York. This place was at the southwestern end of Lake George and was built in 1735.

Until 1759 Canada was unreduced. That year eight thousand men, under Wolfe, fought the terrible battle of the Plains of Abraham, not far from the city of Quebec. Negroes were in this battle in more than one capacity. Among those who served as body servants was Tony Proctor. He was only sixteen years of age at the time of the conflict. He lived to be a very old man, and died in Florida in 1855. Some of the privates were Pompey ———, a native of Guinea, who was sworn in in Capt. Maynard's company; Cuff ———, of Warren, who served His Majesty under Jeffrey Amherst, and Cuff ———, of the Second Massachusetts Regiment of Provincials.

The next year France made an unsuccessful effort to regain her lost territory in America and New Jersey sent her black men into the ranks. By an act of the legislature they were in 1760 enlisted with their masters' consent. The same year an act of Parliament provided for the enlistment of servants as soldiers. For the services of such persons the masters were paid by the recruiting officers out of the public funds.

The war continued until 1763, but the English were then too strong to lose what had fallen into their hands. A treaty of peace, signed that same year, made Great Britain the mistress of all of the land east of the Mississippi River and north of the Iberville in Louisiana. As has been said, there were many Negroes in this war. They came especially from the northern colonies to help the English win their victory. Many were enrolled in the colony of Massachusetts simply as Caesar, and many are the ways of spelling that name, for black men described as privates in muster rolls are reported as Caesar, Caezer, Cesar, Cezar, Sarser, Seazon, Eunta, Ceser, Ceezer, Seasar, Ceasar, Ceazer, Sarser, Seazon and Augustus.

CRISPUS ATTUCKS IN THE BOSTON MASSACRE.

Scarcely had the curtain fallen upon the closing scene of the French and Indian War before the first act of the Revolutionary struggle began, for although five years elapsed between the firing of the guns that were heard around the world from Concord Bridge and the Battle of Bunker Hill, many historians concede that the fight for American independence really began when the blood of Crispus Attucks was shed upon the streets of Boston.

The Stamp Act, duties laid upon glass and tea, the dissolution of the Massachusetts Assembly by the English king, the Billoting Act, which forced the Americans to lodge and feed British troops, were all sources of great aggravation to the colonists, especially to those residing in Boston. They revolted against these acts of tyranny to such a degree that they incurred the displeasure of their king and he determined to humiliate them. To that end, in the fall of 1768, he sent over four regiments of British troops, numbering seven hundred men. These were stationed in Boston, under Gen. Gage. Between the soldiers and the people of the town there were clashes continually, even the boys were not unmolested.

The climax to these rows, which ended on March the fifth, 1770, began three days earlier, when a soldier applied for employment at the rope works of John Gray. This fellow was sent away with rough language, after having been beaten in a boxing match which occurred at his own challenge. Later in the day he returned with several of his comrades to renew the altercation, but they, too, were driven off. The soldiers, upon learning of this matter, felt that an indignity had been placed upon their regiment and determined to meet the citizens in an effort to remove it. They were considerate enough, however, to warn the people for whom they had any friendliness to keep off of the streets. It was not long before the feelings of both populace and soldiers were in a seething state and very unpleasant events occurred during the next two days. Men who should have been in their quarters at night were in the streets after dark harrassing the citizens, both in trade and out-of-door intercourse. Early on the evening of the fifth a quarrel took place between a barber's boy and a redcoat, when the latter was accused by the former of not having paid his bill for a hair cut. The boy received a blow on the head for this taunt which made him cry out with pain. Following this event a number of soldiers came up, threatening to kill every one in sight, and another boy was knocked down. By this time the excitement was so great that the alarm bell at the head of King street was rung. This, of course, brought out a number of people, both citizens and English troops. Partly through the interference of well-disposed officers and partly through the courage of Crispus Attucks, a mulatto, this affray was soon over.

The indignation of the populace was at high pitch, however, and while some of the cooler heads were for going home, many others were for an immediate attack upon the quarters of the main guard, or the "Nest," as they called it, located on the green or common. So bent on avenging their wrongs and "led" by Attucks, the wrathful townfolk pressed on, the crowd growing larger and larger each minute. Many boys and youths fell into line. Some, like the barber's boy, fomenting their anger as they proceeded by the recital of personal affronts from the soldiers. Up what was then King street they went, crying out, "Let us drive out these ribalds. They have no business here." At the custom house the band, still led by the mulatto, assailed the sentinel with snowballs, pieces of ice or anything else that could be used as missles. So furiously did they do this that their victim called for the guard, and the corporal and a few soldiers were sent to protect him. These were met by the patriots, who in warm language dared them to fire. As a result the noise and confusion were terrific. Men howled and swore, and bells rang. The soldiers awaited the order to fire, knowing full well that under existing circumstancs it should come from a civil magistrate. It is impossible to tell whether Attucks and those with him knew this fact or not. At any rate he, with twelve of the men, began to strike upon the muskets of the soldiers with clubs and to taunt them with being afraid to fire and crying to the people behind them, "Be not afraid; they dare not fire. Why do you hesitate? Why do you not kill them? Why not crush them at once?" Whereupon Capt. Preston came up and attempted to disperse the crowd. Attucks struck at the English officer's head, who warded off the blow with his hand. Just then a soldier's musket fell to the ground and Attucks seized it. A struggle followed between the two men for its possession, and the owner was either knocked down or else he fell to the ground. At this time voices in the crowd took up the cry, "Why don't you fire?" Upon hearing these words the soldier, struggling to his feet, fired as he arose, and the brave Crispus, leaning upon a stick, received two balls in each breast. These caused his death. More firing occurred and three others were immediately killed. They were Caldwell, Maverick and Gray. Five persons were dangerously injured and several slightly hurt.

The dead men were regarded as heroes and a public funeral was given them, the rites being celebrated in the most solemn manner as a manifestation of the sorrow and the regret felt by the people for their death. The service for all three* of them was held at the same hour in Faneuil Hall on the eighth of March, the bells of Roxbury, Boston and of Charlestown being tolled meanwhile. The three processions, made up of carriages in which rode distinguished men and friends of the victims, met at King street and wound their way to Middle Burying Ground on Tremont street, a few steps from the head of the Boston Common. Here the bodies were interred in one tomb, located in the extreme northeastern corner of the cemetery.

Very little more than this is known concerning the black hero of this event. He was born about 1723 in the vicinity of Cochetuate Lake, Framingham, Mass., of probably Negro and Indian parentage He escaped from slavery in this locality in 1750. He was a well-proportioned mulatto with curly hair. At the time of his death he was forty-seven years of age.

The spot on which Attucks fell, located on what is now State street, somewhat to the east of the old State House, is today marked by an arrow embedded in the sidewalk. On the Boston Common stands a monument of granite erected in honor of the men who fell in the massacre. One side of this memorial bears this quotation from Daniel Webster, "From that moment we may date the severance of the British Empire," and this one from John Adams, "On that night the foundation of American independence was laid." On the other faces of the monument may be read, respectively, the date of its erection and the name of the fallen heroes, with the time of their death. After the Boston Massacre March fifth was always glorified by patriotic celebrations each year until the Declaration of Independence took its place. Attucks always received due credit for his patriotism on these occasions from even such men as Hancock and Washington, while in 1773 John Adams addressed in the name of the mulatto, the following letter to the Tory governor, Hutchinson, who still continued the persecution of the colonists.

"You shall hear from us with astonishment. You ought to hear from us with horror. You are charged before God and man with our blood. The soldiers were but passionate instruments, mere machines, neither moral nor voluntary instruments, in our destruction, more than the leaden bullets with which we were wounded. You were a free agent. You acted coolly, deliberately, with all that premeditated malice not against us in particular but against the people in general, which in the sight of the law is an ingredient in the composition of murder. You will hear from us hereafter.
(Signed)   CRISPUS ATTUCKS."

*The body of one was claimed by friends and buried out of Boston.

NEGROES IN THE AMERICAN REVOLUTION.

MASSACHUSETTS.

The five years subsequent to the Boston Massacre saw a smouldering fire of sentiment, growing larger and larger in all of the colonies in favor of independence from the mother country. In Massachusetts, by the spring of 1775, preparations had already begun for the war which the provincials felt was inevitable. Military stores had been collected and men drilled upon many village greens. Shortly after midnight on April 18th of that year a detachment of English soldiers left Boston to go to Concord that they might there destroy a supply of cannon, small arms and ammunition stored in that place by the Committee on Public Safety. To prevent this, companies of men ready to respond on the minute, hence called Minute Men, came out of every farm and village along the line of march taken by these troops. Negroes, bond and free, were among this band of defenders. Boston alone had many free colored people and over two thousand slaves at this time, to say nothing of Cambridge and the other towns along the road to Concord. The wrathful Americans met the British, first on Lexington Common, where a short skirmish occurred, in which several of the former lost their lives and the result was a defeat for the colonists. As they took up the march to Concord many recruits entered their ranks. Among them was a Negro, Peter Salem, of Framingham. He entered the ranks of the little band of patriots as a Minute Man, and when they met the foe on Concord Bridge he, with the black man, Samuel Craft, of Newton, and a number of others of their race, helped the sturdy American farmers win a victory which forced the British to retreat to Boston. In that city, by April 28 of the same year, three thousand regulars were blockaded by these farmers.

The Battle of Bunker Hill.

In a very short while the English holdings in Boston were very much strengthened by reinforcements from England, and the Americans realized that it would be to their advantage to have fortified some point from which they might overlook the city and the harbor. Their camp was on the Cambridge Common, and Cambridge lay to the west of Boston, across the Charles River. Of all the points of elevation nearby, Breed's Hill, on the Charlestown side of the stream, was considered most favorable to this end. It happened, then, that on June sixteenth one thousand of the colonials secretly left their camp and proceeded by a mistake to Bunker Hill, there to build a redoubt. When the clock struck the hour of midnight, so swift were their movements that they had already unslung their packs and were stacking their arms. The before-mentioned Peter Salem was there, as were also the black men, Titus Coburn and Seymour Burr, of Andover; Grant Cooper and Cato Howe, the latter all the way up from Plymouth. There was also Charlestown Eads, shouldering his pick with the well-known "spirit of '76." He entered the army at the very beginning of the trouble and was afterwards in Col. Bigelow's company of the Fifteenth Massachusetts. He was not discharged until December 3, 1780. Barzillai Lew, the giant cooper, born at Chelmsford, was there, too. He later became a famous musician in the Continental Army, in the Twenty-seventh Regiment under Capt. Ford. He had served in this capacity in the French and Indian War. He it was who organized for guerrilla warfare at a later period of the struggle a band of Negro men, all of one family, known as Lew's men. He was later in the engagement which took place at Ticonderoga and remained in the ranks until 1777. There also was Sampson Talbert, of Bridgewater, helping to throw up the hillocks on Bunker Hill that warm night in early June. He afterwards spoke of this service as the "hottest day's work he had ever done." These men were all pensioners at the close of the war. So well did the black and the white compatriots work, and so quietly, that the English knew nothing of their nearness until daylight the next day, when the outworks were almost closed. By an army twice the size of their own the Americans were attacked on the 17th day of June, and the terrible battle of Bunker Hill occurred, "in which the dead lay as thick as sheep in the fold," says one writer. Indeed, each army lost nearly a third of its number. Among those who fell on the American side was the Negro, Caesar Brown, of Westford. Twice were the American farmers able to repel the British before they themselves retreated, and this they did only when powder and shot were all gone and there was nothing left with which to fight except butts and barrels of guns. After the brave Warren had fallen, the English mounted the hill in the wake of their commander, Maj. Pitcairn, who as he came, waving his sword, exclaimed, "The day is ours." It was then that the black Peter Salem seized another's gun, his own having been lost in battle, and shot the Englishman, who fell dying in the arms of his son, who was just behind him. For this deed of valor Salem received a contribution from the army and was later presented to Gen. Washington. Salem was born a slave. Besides the engagements already referred to, he was present at the battles of Saratoga and of Stony Point, with many others of his race. He served "as a faithful soldier in the regiment of Col. Nixon." After the war was over he resided a long time in Leisester, Massachusetts, on a road named in his honor, leading to Auburn. He finally removed to his native town, Framingham, where he died August 16, 1816. There he is buried in an old cemetery. In 1882, at a cost of one hundred and fifty dollars, the townfolks erected a monument three feet high, of Middlesex granite, in his honor. This gives information concerning the battles in which he fought and calls him a "Soldier of the Revolution." For many years an old bank in Charlestown, the Monumental, as well as the Freedmen's Bank of Boston, commemorated his deed by placing his picture upon their bank notes. A painting of the battle of Bunker Hill, made by an eye witness, shows the likeness of Salem. Among the other black men present at the battle of Bunker Hill were Caesar Basom, of Westford; Alexander Eames, of Boston; Saesar Jahar, of Natick; Cuff Blanchard and Caesar Post, of Andover, and ———— Gushar, of Framingham. Caesar Basom lost his lie in the engagement. He was at first a private in the company of Capt. John Mino, and marched with these men to Lexington from Westford. In the action on Bunker Hill he was in the company of Capt. Weyman. As he fired his last charge of powder, exclaiming, "Now, Caesar, give them some more," he was shot and fell dead into the trenches. He was a stripling of twenty-two. Another colored man who distinguished himself in the battle fought on the little hill at Charlestown was Salem Poor. He killed Lieut. Col. Abercrombie, of the British Regulars, as the latter sprang on the redoubt and shouted, "Surrender, you rebels." A petition in favor of Salem Poor was sent to the general court of Massachusetts six months after the battle was fought, signed by some of the principal officers. It read as follows:

"The subscribers beg leave to report to your Honorable House, which we do in justice to the character of so brave a man, that under our own observation we declare that a Negro, called Salem Poor, of Col. Fry's regiment, Capt. Eames' company, in the late battle of Charlestown, behaved like an experienced officer, as well as an excellent soldier. To set forth the particulars of his conduct would be tedious. We only beg leave to say, in the person of the said Negro is set forth a brave and gallant soldier. The reward due so great and distinguished a character we submit to Congress.

JONAH BREW, *Colonel,*
EPHM COREY, *Lieutenant,*
JOSHUA ROW, *Lieutenant,*
JONAS RICHARDSON, *Captain,*
JOSIAH FOSTER, *Captain,*
JOHN .MORTON, *Sergeant,*
THOMAS NIXON, *Lieut. Colonel,*
JOSEPH BARKER, *Lieutenant,*
WILLIAM PRESCOTT, *Colonel,*
ELIAPHALETT BODWELL,' *Sergeant,*
EBENEZER VARNUM, *2nd Lieutenant,*
WILLIAM H. VALLARD, *Captain,*
RICHARD WALSH, *Lieutenant,*
WILLIAM SMITH, *Captain.*

"In council, December 21, 1775. Read and sent down.

"PEREZ MORTON, *Secretary.*"

Salem Poor did duty at Fort George, Ticonderoga, Valley Forge and White Plains. His term of enlistment did not expire untl 1780.

Negroes Excluded From and Re-Enlisted in the Army.

The colonists, realizing that war was upon them, bent every effort that theirs might be the victory at its close. Washington took command of the Continental Army on July 3, 1775. There he found much to do in the way of organization. In its ranks, as has already been said, were many Negroes. Very soon the consistency of employing slaves in the fight for liberty became a much debated question on the part of those in authority. So, despite their manifestations of courage at Lexington, Concord and Bunker Hill, a committee appointed to consider the matter resolved that all black men be excluded from the army, except those who were free, declaring that a participation in this fight'by any others would be a reflection on the honor of the colony. On the passage of this act many slaves were emancipated that they might enlist, and this they did in very large numbers. In a short time objection was again raised to the presence of Negroes in the army, and a committee, made up of Benjamin Franklin, Benjamin Harrison, Thomas Kench and the Deputy Governors of Rhode Island and Connecticut, which convened October, 1775, to consider the condition of the army and to plan for its improvement, recommended that all black men be excluded from its ranks. Washington endorsed this decision. This act, however, met strong protest from the officers and men who had served with persons of color, to say nothing of the expressions of dissatisfaction made by the latter themselves. They even appealed for the annulment of this law. About this time an affair occurred in Virginia which materially changed things in Massachusetts as far as black soldiers were concerned. This was the hearty response on the part of black men to an invitation, through a proclamation of Lord Dunmore, the Tory governor of that colony, to its slaves to enter the Ministerial Army with the promise of freedom. These men distinguished themselves like soldiers at the battle of Kemp's Landing, the present site of Kempville, Virginia, located between Norfolk and the sea. This engagement occurred between the Loyalists and the Federalists. These facts being made known to the Commander-in-chief of the American Army, he decided to ignore the exclusion act and ordered that Negroes be re-enlisted, unless otherwise so directed by Congress. Thus it came about that they were re-employed and Congress endorsed this policy on January 16, 1776, by an act of legislation which was never thereafter set aside. Through all the ensuing years of the war they entered the ranks and not a regiment was seen in which there was not a goodly number "of the able-bodied, strong fellows."

Fortifications at Dorchester and Castle Island.

In the first winter of the war occurred the Seige of Boston. A number of the boats of the enemy were then in the harbor, whose waters roared at the end of many of the streets of Boston. That the foe might not make a contemplated landing at Dorchester, a village adjoining this city, the Americans decided to make a fortification there. So one night early in March they sent a force whose vanguard numbered eight hundred men with tools and carts to the highlands overlooking Dorchester Bay. These men, many of whom were Negroes, among them being Primus Hall and James Easton, of Bridgewater, under the direction of Putnam, piled up apple boughs from the nearby orchards to make hurdles and fascines. On these they set bales of hay, packing them tightly to make them cannon-proof. They had also not far away a collection of barrels of sand and stones which they intended to roll down upon the enemy should they come near enough from their ships in the harbor. It was this action that made Gen. Howe's position in Boston untenable.

At this period Negroes also aided in throwing up fortifications at Castle Island, another point in the Boston Harbor,

Separate Companies of Negroes.

In the spring of the same year Thomas Kench, then an officer in the regiment of artillery, stationed at Castle Island, wished to raise and have command of a body of two or three hundred colored men, "Sergeants, corporals, drummers and fifers," as he said, "all to be of the same race." These men were to be set free at the end of their services. Concerning the matter, he addressed the following letter to the General Assembly:

"* * * And what I refer to is Negroes. We have divers of them in our service, mixed with white men. But I think it would be more proper to raise a body by themselves than to have them intermixed with white men, and their ambition would be entirely to outdo the men in every measure that the fortune of war causes a soldier to endure. And I could rely with dependence on them in the field of battle, or to any post that I was sent to defend with them, and they would think themselves happy could they gain their freedom by bearing a part of subduing the enemy that is invading our land and thus secure a peaceful inheritance. The method that I would point out of raising a detachment of Negroes is that a company should consist of one hundred, including a commissioned officer, and that the command should be white and consist of one captain, one captain-lieutenant, two second lieutenants, two orderly sergeants, all white, and three sergeants, four corporals, two drummers and fifers, all black, and eighty-four rank and file. These should engage to serve to the end of the war and then be free men."

A committee of both houses of legislature, acting upon this letter, advised its adoption. It, however, came about that Kench at no time ever had command of a colored company, and yet one or two companies of this kind were created. Samuel Lawrence, of Groton, had charge of one of these, whose courage, fidelity and military discipline won a high degree of respect for them from their leader. Once while in an engagement he was surrounded by the enemy who was about to capture him. His brave followers, discovering his plight, rushed to his rescue and succeeded in saving their leader. For this deed of theirs Lawrence showed special consideration to all of the members of their race whom he happened to meet in the future. The County of Barnstable, Massachusetts, furnished a number of black men to serve in the Revolutionary

War. These men were of mixed blood, Indian and African. They formed a separate company and all save one lost their lives before the conflict ended. Among them were Francis Websquish, Samuel Moses, Demps Squibbs, Mark Negro, Tom Caesar, Joseph Ashur, James Keeter, Joseph Keeter, Daniel Pockknitz and Joe Rimmon.

There was also another colored company commanded by a man of color by the name of Middleton. He was a noted horse breaker. These men, who called themselves the Bucks of America, rendered such meritorious service that at the close of the war they received a banner. This was presented to them by Gen. Hancock. When on a march to a neighboring town to a collation to which they had been invited they were asked to stop in front of the governor's mansion in Boston, and that gentleman and his son came out of the house and presented the banner. Their prize is yet in existence. While it was probably a cream-colored silk, it is now of a buff color. It is five feet, three inches long and three and one-half feet wide. In the upper left-hand corner there are thirteen golden stars upon a blue field. In the center is painted a pine tree, under which, in the act of leaping, is a brown buck. Above the tree is a short scroll which bears the initials "J. G. W. H."* Below it is a long open scroll which stretches very nearly the full length of the design. Upon its blue field the words "Bucks of America" are printed. The flag or banner was undoubtedly painted by hand and is an excellent sample of the artistic handwork done in colonial days.

Among the many blacks who fought in ranks with white men were Abel Benson, a farmer's boy of sixteen, who enlisted in Framingham and served three years; Tony Clark, of Billeirica, who enlisted at the age of nineteen and served from 1776 to 1788; the two Plys, of Rochester, who were likely related, and Bedunah Moses, of Springfield, who took part in the capture of Peekskill, New York, and did extra duty under Gen. Glover. There, too, was Pomp Jackson, liberated for the consideration of five shillings, which he paid to his master himself in June, 1776. He served through the entire war. At its close he settled in Andover, near a pond ever since then called "Pomp's Pond." A black member of Washington's bodyguard from the Bay State was Tobias Gilmore. He enlisted as a private in 1776, in the regiment of Col. George Williams. Gilmore was born an African prince. His native name was Shilbogee Turry-Werry. He was sold on the auction block at Newport as a slave to Capt. Gilmore, of Taunton, from whose home he entered the war as a substitute in order to secure his freedom. On

*Hancock's initials.

his discharge from the army, as a reward for faithful service, he received a section of land and a cannon. Each Independence Day it was Tobias' custom to take the cannon to the Taunton Green and fire once for each of the thirteen original states and once for "Massa Washington." He put an end to his patriotic demonstrations only when a man's arm was shot off. He then said he "guessed he'd better stop," and presented the gun to the historical society, whose property it is today.* In their museum may be seen also a liberty cap and a blue coat trimmed with buff. These articles are a part of the uniform worn by Tobias Gilmore in the Revolutionary War. On the red cap are the words, "Federalism and Liberty," inscribed in white letters on a blue ground.

VERMONT.

Slavery as an institution never reached any importance in Vermont, for by the census of 1790 there were only seventeen bond men in this state. Here, as elsewhere, however, early in the Revolutionary struggle black men were set free that they might enlist and were given a certificate of manumission by their masters, who in turn received the bounty money paid for them by the state.

NEW HAMPSHIRE.

While the number of Negroes residing in the state of New Hampshire was always very small, many of those who were there were called upon to do duty in the time of the War for American Independence. By an act passed early in the history of the conflict black men entered the ranks of the colonial army. Among these were Jude Hall, born in Exeter. He served eight years in all, and fought in a great number of battles, beginning with that on Bunker Hill. Until the day of his death he was known as "Old Rock." Lemuel Haines was another native of this state who enrolled as a Minute Man as early as 1774, when preparations for the war to come were just beginning to go forward. He was at the Battle of Lexington and later became a volunteer in the ranks of the regulars. He took part in the expedition to Ticonderoga against Burgoyne in 1777. He remained in the service until the war ended. There, too, was Boston Pickering, who enlisted as a lad of twenty in the first regiment of militia of New Hampshire.

*1918.

RHODE ISLAND.

The Battle of Fort Mercer or Red Bank.

In 1777, after the Battle of Brandywine, the British planned to clear out the forts, fortifications and flotilla placed on the Delaware River by the Americans. This thing they very much desired to do in the hope of establishing communications between their fleets and that part of their army occupying Philadelphia. To this end they decided to storm Fort Mifflin and Fort Mercer, both located in New Jersey. The latter was on the side of the river at what is now the town of Red Bank, and was rather important because it protected the stream. At this time two Rhode Island regiments under Col. Greene and belonging to that part of the army supervised by Gen. Varnum, were stationed at this place. On October twenty-first Count Donup, with four batalions of Hessians, crossed the Delaware at Cooper's Ferry and marched to Fort Mercer. On the way they met an old Negro called "Old Mitch," whom they tried to secure as a guide to the American stronghold, but in this they were unsuccessful. They came upon the place, however, on the morning of the twenty-second. It was defended by four hundred and twenty men. A Hessian officer approached the fort and ordered its surrender in the name of the English king. Col. Greene refused to obey and his refusal was reported to Dunop. The attack upon the fortification began that afternoon. The Americans left the north side of the fort late in the day. When this fact was discovered by the enemy they rushed triumphantly into the place under the impression that the former had deserted it. Just as they were about to place their flag upon the merlon* of the ramparts they were surprised by a shower of grape shot and musket balls from the embrasures which annihilated them. Another division, under Col. Dunop himself, received the same sort of treatment on the south side of Fort Mercer, thereby suffering a terrible loss through the rapid fire of the Americans. The commander was left upon the field mortally wounded. A large number of the men with Col. Greene at this time were either blacks or mulattos, who by this battle helped to bring to a close the efforts of the British to approach any further inland against Washington before the beginning of the winter. This was very fortunate, for the American army was at that time undergoing many hardships. During the bombardment "Old Mitch" lay hidden in a pile of straw not far away from the fort.

———————

*A battlement.

Separate Rhode Island Regiments.

In order to raise her required quota it came about the next year (1778) that Rhode Island, at the request of Gen. Varnum, formed a battalion composed entirely of Negroes. These men numbered some three hundred black and mulatto slaves. The legislative act calling them into service provided that these soldiers should enjoy all the compensation given to white soldiers, that they should serve through the war, and that their masters should be relieved of all future responsibility for their support should they be disabled or live to advanced age. The state, in either of these cases, was to assume their care. It also arranged for their appraisement and for a compensation which their masters were to receive upon their entering the army. This battalion distinguished itself more than once, but it attained its crowning glory in the Battle of Rhode Island, fought on hills and in dales around Providence and Newport. It was on a hot summer day in August, 1778, that they went into this battle. The English were assisted by their famous hired soldiers, the Hessians. These were a body of Germans from Hesse Cassel, Germany. These men were very brave and very fierce fighters. At one point they charged down the hill with such force as to almost carry the redoubt. It was in repelling these furious onsets that the newly raised regiments under Col. Greene distinguished themselves by deeds of desperate valor. "They three times drove back the Hessians, and so determined were they in these successive charges that the day after the battle the Hessian colonel upon whom that duty devolved applied to exchange his command and go to New York because he dared not again lead his regiment lest his men should kill him for having occasioned them so grave a loss." Lafayette called this the best-fought action of the war. The slaughter was terrible. The British lost thirteen hundred, the Americans two hundred and eleven men. This engagement enabled the Americans to leave the island, not a bit too soon, for early the next morning the English were reinforced by a large fleet commanded by Sir Henry Clinton. A part of the Rhode Island Negro battalion came in prominently for heroism on May 14, 1781, at Pont's Bridge, on the Croton River, in the state of New York. Here some of these men defended their beloved Col. Greene so well that it was only over their dead bodies that the enemy reached and murderd him. In February, 1783, some of them went with a body of New York troops, under Col. Willett, to attack a British trading point on Lake Ontario. Through the treachery or ignorance of an Indian this undertaking was unsuccessful. These men had a very good appearance. It is said that they did not receive their promised bounty money, but were told to accept their freedom instead of it. They did not secure the allowance due them such as was given to white soldiers, but were deprived of their wages by means of forged orders. Among them were Scipio Brown, Thomas Brown, Prince Vaughan, Sampson Hazard, Guy Watson, Richard Rhodes, Henry Taber, Cuff Green, Thomas Rhodes, Blato Green, Prince Green, Prince Jenks, Reubin Roberts, Philo Phillips, Caesar Powers, York Chaplin, Ichabod Northrup, Richard Cousins (fifer).

The Capture of Gen. Prescott.

In connection with the services of colored men of Rhode Island must be given the story of Prince Whipple, or Jack Sissons, as he is sometimes called. Several diaries of the Revolution prove beyond a doubt that this black man helped to capture the English general, Prescott, July 9, 1777. It happened that some time before this date Gen. Lee had been ordered to bring his detachment of the army into the immediate vicinity of Philadelphia. This he had failed to do and had established his headquarters in the mountains of New Jersey at Basken Ridge, about twenty miles from a British camp. Feeling that he was so far away from the enemy that he needed to use no precautions for his safety, he retained only a small bodyguard near him, while the main body of his troops were in camp several miles away. The British learned of this fact through Tories, and overcoming his sentinels Gen. Harcourt easily brought about Lee's arrest and conducted him, a prisoner, to British headquarters in New York, where he was closely confined. The military skill of this American officer was so highly esteemed by his countrymen that his capture caused the greatest consternation and regret among them, and they greatly desired his release. In order to secure this it was planned to take a man of equal rank from the foe, that Lee might be set free through an exchange of prisoners. To this end Lieut. Barton designed the seizure of Gen. Prescott, who had charge of the British forces on Rhode Island. He had landed a large number of troops at Newport in December, 1776, that they might be retained there to operate against the New England States. Finding out through a deserter from the British ranks the exact location of the English general, Barton, accompanied by forty men, one at least of whom was a Negro, started on his expedition. The Americans landed within five miles of the place, and when near the residence of a Quaker, with whom the general was staying, Barton, with Prince Whipple and a few others of his men, proceeded to the house, having left his main party in concealment. The sentinel at the door challenged him, but after a short parley he was overpow<

ered and ordered, upon pain of death, to be silent. The rest of the men, answering to an expected given signal, then surrounded the dwelling. The Negro, with two strokes of his head, forced an entry into the house, and the landlord then came upon the scene. Questioned as to the whereabouts of Prescott, he refused to give any information concerning the Englishman, but when threatened with death he pointed to the door of the officer's room. This was at once opened by Prince Whipple through the same process that he had used upon the front door. The general was then informed that he was a prisoner and he surrendered without resistance to the Americans. Through his capture Lee was released. Jack Sisson, or Prince Whipple, who certainly helped to bring this event to pass, was a slave, the property of Gen. Whipple, of the American army. He was born in Africa, was kidnapped and sold in Baltimore. It is his likeness that is often seen in old paintings of Washington crossing the Delaware.

CONNECTICUT.

Many Connecticut Negroes entered the army during the War of the Revolution. Long after the struggle was over almost every white family had its tradition of a slave or a servant who had either been killed in some battle, or who, having served through the war, had come home to tell stories of hard fighting and to be pensioned. A number of these men were enlisted as substitutes in place of their masters. The recruiting officer lost little time inquiring if his recruits were white or black, and he did not question their legal status if they were able-bodied. Most of these men were placed in the ranks with white men, but in the year 1777 the advisability of raising companies of colored troops was discussed in the General Assembly of this state, and a committee was appointed to consider the matter. The result of the deliberation of this body was a recommendation that Negro and mulatto slaves whose masters were to be paid the sum of their appraisement, and who themselves upon enlisting would become free, should be formed into a separate company. Following this a company of fifty-six men was organized in this state. They were commanded by Col. Humphrey, who volunteered to do so after many other officers, upon request, had refused to take charge of them. They were in Butler's regiment, in that division of the army over which Maj. Laurens had charge. "They conducted themselves with fidelity and efficiency through the war." Their names are as follows:

Jack Arabus, Ned Fields, Louis Martin, Peter Mix, Prince George, Shugael Johnson, Dick Violet, Gamaliel Bagden, Ned Freedom, Congo Zado, Pomp Liberty, Sharp Rogers, Cuff Freeman, Andrew Jack, Peter Lyon, Daniel Bradley, Sharp Camp, Solomon Sowtice, Pomp Cyrus, John Cleveland, Phineas Strong, Juba Freeman, Philo Freeman, Prince Crosbee, Jack Little, Alex Judd, Leut Munson, Ezekiel Tupham, Peter Gibbs, Cuff Liberty, Job Caesar, Juba Dyer, Peter Morando, Samson Cuff, Dick Freeman, Joe Otis, Cato Wilbrow, Pomp Freeman, Hector Williams, Isaac Higgins, Caesar Chapman, Cato Robinson, Tim Caesar, Bill Soweis, Caesar Bagden, Herman Rogers, Tom Freeman, Prince Johnson, Harry Williams, John Rogers, John Ball, John McLean, Jesse Vose, Pomp McCuff, James Dinah, Brewster Baker.

While it is impossible to know the exact number, some. hundreds of dark men enlisted in this state in mixed companies, among these were Sambo Lathon, or Lambert, and Jordan Freeman, both of whom fought with the bravest at Groton after the Americans had been forced to retreat to that place from New London. In September, 1778, after a terrible engagement at Fort Griswold, on the heights of Groton, the fortification was surrendered by Col. Ledyard, the commander in charge. The English officer who took the fort committed the unwarrantable atrocity of stabbing him. It was Lathon who quickly avenged this unusual act by running his bayonet through the Briton. For this deed he received thirty thrusts from the enemy's bayonets. On the same occasion Jordan Freeman received the victorious Maj. Montgomery on his pike as the latter was lifted over the wall of the fortress.

Many slaves, who entered the conflict under a promise of freedom, had to petition the Connecticut Legislature for the same after it was over. Nineteen of them were not pensioned until the year 1818. One of these was Prime Babcock, who held a discharge in the handwriting of Washington.

New York.

Battle of Stony Point.

There were many desirable places for fortifications on the Hudson River. One of these was at Stony Point, on the west side of the stream, on a great highway connecting the Middle and the New England States. Nature had protected this point on three sides by the river and on the fourth by a swamp which could be crossed at low tide by a causeway. The Americans had lost a stronghold here in 1777, and they were very desirous of regaining it. Gen. Anthony Wayne was appointed by Washington for this exploit. Learning that Pompey Lamb, a Negro living on a nearby farm, visited the

fort regularly to sell fresh vegetables and berries, Wayne decided
to employ him as a spy. Contact with this slave had very much
pleased the English officers. This was due to his low prices, as well
as to his engaging manner, and this doubtless facilitated his efforts
to closely observe the plan of the fortification. At first he made only
daytime trips, but acting upon the instruction of the officer who had
employed him and that of his master, Capt. Lamb, he told the British that as he hereafter had to hoe corn he could no longer come in
the day, but would serve them at night if given a pass. Unwilling
to lose his fresh vegetables, the English gave him their countersign,
"The fort is our own," that he might pass the guards at any time he
was able to come.

On the night of July 15th, having killed all the dogs in the neighborhood that their bark might not arouse suspicion, the Americans made an attack upon the fort. First came Pompey, carrying
his fruit and vegetables, accompanied by two soldiers disguised as
farmers. He engaged the first sentinel he met in conversation, giving him some fruit meanwhile. The disguised soldiers seized and
gagged this man, and soon after a second sentinel was similarly
treated. By this means the causeway was left unprotected, and
Anthony Wayne and the rest of his men, hidden not far away, were
enabled to make an entry into the fortification. So silently did they
ascend the cliff that their presence was not known until they were
within pistol range of the guards on the highland. Here a skirmish
occurred which awoke the entire fort. The Americans forced their
way in amidst a terrible fire. At the close of the battle the garrison
of six hundred men was surrendered by Capt. de Fleurry. For
his deed Pompey received a horse from his master and was never
required by him to work again. In the ranks of the Americans at
this time were several Negroes, one of whom was "Father Stanup."
He was wounded and left on the field for dead. He, however, re-
covered, and died many years later, near Urbana, in Champagne
County, Ohio. Peter Salem, of Bunker Hill, was also in this battle.

On March 20, 1781, the legislature of New York passed an act
worded as follows:
"Sec. 6. And be it further enacted by the authority of
the aforesaid that any person who shall deliver one or more
of his or her ablebodied slaves to any one in office, as aforesaid, to serve in either of the said regiments, or independent
corps, and produce a certificate thereof signed by any persons authorized to muster and receive the men to be raised
by this act and produce such certificate to the Surveyor General, shall for every male slave so mustered and entered, as
aforesaid, be entitled to the location and grant of one right

in manner as by and in this act is directed shall be and hereby is discharged from any further maintenance of such slave, any law to the contrary notwithstanding. And such slave so entered as aforesaid, who shall serve for the term of three years, or until regularly discharged, shall immediately after such service or discharge be and is hereby declared to be a free man of this state."

This statute provided for the raising of two separate regiments of men of color from the empire state. How many entered the army through its enactment it seems impossible to tell, yet at the same time it is obvious that black men in goodly numbers served their country here as elsewhere.

The name of "Negro Tom" appears as early as March 18, 1776, on the rolls of the Orangetown, New York, regiment, as a drummer in the company of Capt. Egbert. Phillip Field is mentioned as having enlisted April 15, 1777, in the Second New York Regiment. This man was a slave, of Duchess County, New York. He died in Valley Forge, August, 1778. These facts prove indisputably that black men of New York entered the American army at the very earliest period of the strife. This is not at all surprising when it is recalled that on July 21, 1776, the English were reported to have collected in their ranks on Staten Island alone, eight hundred slaves, the property of American masters. These men had gone over to assist the enemy with the promise of receiving their freedom. To prevent any more of this, as well as to strengthen their own forces, the Americans early saw the necessity of enlisting the blacks in this state.

Many Negroes fell in the Battle of Long Island. This engagement occurred in August, 1776. It was an effort made by the British to take the fortifications situated on Brooklyn Heights with the hope of finally securing New York City. To this end they landed a force of twenty thousand men, English and Hessians, the latter under Gen. De Heister, at Sandy Hook and at Gravesend Cove, the last-named place near the present site of Fort Hamilton. The foe advanced through four passes upon the American position, which was held by a force of some ten thousand men. A fierce fight occurred on the road to Flatbush, in which a part of the colonial army was badly crippled. Later all of the American forces were forced to join in a midnight flight across the river to New York.

Burgoyne's Surrender.

Gen. Burgoyne planned to seize Albany in the early fall of 1777, boasting that he would eat his Christmas dinner in that city. It was his hope to make a junction with the forces of Great Britain, stationed in various parts of this section, by forcing his way to the Hudson River from Upper New York. Toward the accomplishment of this effort he was successful in capturing Crown Point and the artillery at Ticonderoga that Gen. Sinclair was trying to move. He was able also to force the Americans to leave the latter place. Reaching Fort Edward, a point on the Hudson, he sent a force of Hessians into Vermont to capture some military stores and horses there belonging to the colonials. The result of this expedition was the Battle of Bennington, fought by the Americans under Stark, which resulted in a complete defeat for the enemy. Seven hundred of the men were taken prisoners. When Stark asked for a rope to secure some of these, a Mrs. Robinson, of whom he made the request, said she would give the last one belonging to her bedstead if her Negro slave might harness up her old mare and lead the British, Hessian and Tory captives away. The general acquiesced, and a black man led a part of the left wing of Burgoyne's army over the state line down the road leading to Boston. Burgoyne led his remaining forces to Stillwater, New York, a Hudson River village, near which place, on Bemis Heights, on September 19th, he was hotly attacked by white and by black Americans. At the close of this battle he was forced to surrender. A Negro who aided in bringing about this result was Ebenezer Hills, born a slave in Connecticut. This man was also at the Battle of Saratoga, and died at an advanced age in Vienna, New York.

NEW JERSEY.

It is probable that black men of New Jersey went into the conflict at the very first call to arms, for when facilitated by the parting of the ice at McConkey's Ferry Washington crossed the Delaware on that memorable Christmas night, the "mulatto" Oliver Cromwell was there, with others of his race, to take part in the Battle of Trenton on the next day. This battle resulted in a victory for the continentals, who took about a thousand prisoners from the foe. When describing it Cromwell often said, "We knocked the British about quite lively." This man was a farmer. He enlisted in the company of Capt. Loney, Second Regiment, New Jersey, under Col. Israel Shreeve. He remained in the army until the war was over, serving in all about six years and nine months, and receiving a discharge in Washington's own handwriting   He was also in the Battles of Brandywine and of Monmouth. At the end of the war he became a pensioner, receiving ninety-six dollars a year. In many old paintings of the famous passage across the Delaware may be seen the likeness of a Negro near the commander-in-chief in the fore of the boat. The original was Prince Whipple, an African chief, who had been sent to America by his father to be educated, but who had been sold. instead as a slave in Baltimore to Gen. Whipple by the very captain on whose ship he sailed from his native home. He entered the war with his master, but was emancipated before its close.

The Battles of Brandywine and Monmouth.

All of the cities on the Atlantic coast were in turn viewed with covetous eyes by the British. They desired very greatly to capture Philadelphia and fought several battles to this end. Among them was one known as the Battle of Brandywine, which occurred September 11, 1777, on the steep banks of a stream bearing that name. The black men, Brazaillai Lew and Sanford Talbert, were in this engagement.

The Battle of Monmouth.

The Battle of Monmouth was another contest fought to prevent the British from seizing the City of Brotherly Love. This engagement took place when the English, under Gen. Clinton, on their way to New York, met the Americans near the village of Monmouth, on Wrennock Creek, June 28, 1778. It appeared in the early part of the fight that the enemy would be victorious, for much apathy was manifested on the part of the Americans, due, it is said, to the treachery of one of Washington's aides. At any rate, whether this be true or not, the commander-in-chief, after seeing many of his colonels passing in swift retreat from the onslaught of their opponents, was forced to conduct the rally in person, and affairs then took a turn in favor of the colonists. In this engagement, and to whom much of its success was due, were over seven hundred black men, standing side by side with the other Americans. They belonged not only to New Jersey but to several other sections of the country, as a glance at the army return, made public a few months later, will show:

RETURN OF NEGROES IN THE ARMY, 24th AUG., 1778.

Brigades.	Present.	Sick-Absent.	On Command.	Total.
North Carolina	42	10	6	58
Woodford	36	3	1	40
Muhlenburg	64	26	8	98
Smallwood	20	3	1	24
2nd Maryland	DC	15	2	60
Wayne	2	--	—	2
2nd Maryland	33	1	1	35
Clinton	33	2	4	39
Parsons	117	12	19	148
Huntington	56	2	4	62
Nixon	26	—	1	27
Patterson	64	13	12	89
Late Learned	34	4	8	46
Poor	16	7	4	27
	586	98	71	755

Alexander Scammel, Adjutant General.

One of these men was Samuel Charlton, a native of New Jersey. He entered the service as a substitute for his master. At first he was only a teamster, but in this engagement he gave artillery service, and stood very near the famous Molly Pitcher when she took her wounded husband's place at the cannon. Charlton's conduct brought him personal notice from Washington. He was in several other battles in this state.

New Jersey seems to have offered no resistance to the entrance of her men of color into the army. The master's consent was necessary before a slave could enlist, it is true, but only that the former might not be deprived of the services of his bondman without the equivalent in money. In 1784 the legislature of this state set free all slaves who had taken part in the American Revolution, liberating also those doing war service belonging to Tory masters. Among these were Peter Williams, who was taken by his master into the British lines. He escaped and served a while with the state troops. Later he entered the ranks of the continental army, where he remained until the war was over. Cato ———, of the same town, became free under like conditions. He was liberated by a special act passed in 1789, which declared he had rendered "essential service, both to the state and to the United States in time of war." Beside these there was Prime ———, of Princeton. He was emancipated because "He was entitled to special notice from the legislature" for reasons similar to those which gave Cato his liberty.

PENNSYLVANIA.

As early as 1777, and perhaps sooner, Negroes of Pennsylvania had enlisted in the struggle which freed the colonists from the rule of Great Britain. In that year there were thirty-three blacks in the 2nd Regiment of Pennsylvania under Washington just after the famous Battle of Monmouth, and state records prove conclusively that all during the early period of the war bond servants, as slaves were here called, were enlisted even without their masters' consent, although this was against the law. Freemen, without a doubt, were taken into the army to aid the colonials during the entire period of the war.

MARYLAND.

Maryland was not unlike her sister colonies in calling upon Negroes to aid her in the struggle for independence. A field return of Negroes in the main army in August, 1778, shows that at that time there were sixty blacks in the Second Maryland Brigade. By an act passed in 1780 all males previously exempted (Negroes) were made liable to draft, and all able-bodied slaves were recruited, with their own or their masters' consent. The following year, when only a part of a certain quota called for months before had been raised, two extra battalions were ordered added to the army by the enlistment of free blacks (of whom there were not a few in this state), as well as others, over the age of sixteen, if idle or without means of support or family. This same year (1781) the legislature voted on the motion of John Calwalader in order to raise two regiments of a grant of unappropriated land be given every slave holder for each able-bodied slave that he or she enlisted. This act relieved the master from further responsibility for the black who was to be free at the end of three years' service unless regularly discharged before then. These men were to be incorporated with the rest of the army and some of them were doubtless at the Battle of Camden. It was in this engagement, occurring in South Carolina in 1780, that the Maryland and Delaware troops displayed much valor, although the enemy won the day. Baron De Kalb was mortally wounded at this time. Among these men of Maryland was Thomas Holland, a

Negro, of Dorset County. He and his uncle served together in the war and they were attached to the regiment of Col. Charles Goldberg.

VIRGINIA.

Almost at the very beginning of the Revolutionary War Lord Dunmore, the Royalist Governor of Virginia, issued a proclamation in which he invited slaves to enter the ministerial army. Very many responded to his call. These people were inspired to leave their masters by the hope of receiving their freedom, which was promised them by the English. The enlistment of Negroes in the ranks of the Tories caused great concern in the minds of the Federalists who, in their turn, made an apeal to them to stand by their true friends. This appeal was printed in a newspaper of Williamsburg, Virginia, on November 23, in the year 1776, and read:

"CAUTION TO NEGROES."

"The second class of people for whose sake a few remarks upon this proclamation seem necessary is the Negroes. They have been flattered with their freedom if they be able to bear arms and will speedily join Lord Dunmore's troops. To none of them is freedom promised but to such as are able to do Lord Dunmore's service. The aged, the infirm, the women, the children are still to remain the property of their masters, who will be provoked to severity should part of their slaves desert them. Lord Dunmore's declaration, then, is a cruel declaration to the Negroes. He does not pretend to make it out of any tenderness to them, but solely on his own account, and should it meet with success it leaves by far the greater number at the mercy of an enraged and injured people. But should there be any among the Negroes weak enough to believe that Lord Dunmore intends to do them a kindness and wicked enough to provoke the fury of the Americans against their defenseless fathers and mothers, their wives, their women, and their children, let them only consider the difficulty of effecting their escape and what they must expect to suffer if they fall into the hands of the Americans. Let them consider further what must be their fate if the English prove conquerors. If we can judge the future from the past it will not be much mended. Long have the Americans, moved by compassion and actuated by sound policy, endeavored to stop the progress of slavery. Our assemblies have repeatedly passed acts laying heavy duties upon importing Negroes, by which they meant altogether to prevent the horrid traffic. But their humane intentions have been as often frustrated by the cruelty and covetousness of a set of English merchants who prevailed upon the king to repeal our kind and merciful act, little, indeed, to his credit or humanity. Can it be supposed that the Negroes will be better used by the English, who have always encouraged and upheld this slavery, than by their present masters who pity their condition, who wish in general to make it as easy and comfortable as possible, and who would, were it in their power or were they permitted, not only prevent any more Negroes from losing their freedom but restore it to such as have lost it already? No, the ends of Lord Dunmore and his party being answered, they would either give up the offending Negroes to the rigor of the law they have broken or sell them in the West Indies, where every year they sell many thousands of their miserable brethren, to perish either by the inclemency of the weather or through the cruelty of barbarous masters. Be not then, ye Negroes, tempted by this proclamation to ruin yourselves. I have given you a faithful view of what you are to expect, and declare before God in doing it I have considered your welfare as well as that of the country. Whether you will profit by my advice I cannot tell, but this I know, that whether we suffer or not, if you desert us you certainly will."

For a time many slaves entered the British ranks, in spite of the warning at the end of this appeal. A number of them "acquitted themselves like soldiers" in the Battle of Kemp's Landing, in the fall of 1776. Indeed, so great was their desertion of their masters that the latter saw fit to offer pardon to all who would return to them within ten days, in the following terms:

"Whereas, Lord Dunmore, by his proclamation dated on board the ship William, off Norfolk, the seventh day of November, 1776, hath offered freedom to such able-bodied slaves as are willing to join him and take up arms against the good people of this colony, giving thereby encouragement to a general insurrection which may induce the necessity of inflicting the severest punishment upon these unhappy people, already deluded by his base and insiduous arts, and whereas, by an act of the General Assembly, now in force in this colony, it is enacted that all Negro or other slaves conspiring to rebel or make insurrection shall suffer death and be excluded of all benefit of clergy, we think it proper to declare that all slaves who have been or shall be seduced by his lordship's proclamation or other arts to desert their masters' service and take up arms against the inhabitants of this colony, shall be liable to such punishment as shall hereafter be directed by general convention. And to that end, that all such who have taken this unlawful and wicked step may return in safety to their duty and escape the punishment due their crimes, we hereby promise pardon to them, they surrendering themselves to Col. William Woodward or any other commander of our troops, and not appearing in arms after the publication hereof. And we do further recommend it to all humane and benevolent persons in this colony to explain and make known this, our offer of mercy to those unfortunate people."

Shortly after this the exodus into the ranks of the English began to decrease, for it developed that many of the blacks, instead of being used as soldiers, were being sold into slavery in the West Indies by the British.

Many free Negroes entered the ranks of the Colonial Army before 1777. Slaves also went in as substitutes, and so many ran away and pretended to be free, that they might enlist, that in this year an act was passed by which all Negroes were compelled to show certificates of freedom before being taken into the army. A little later those who were above the age of thirty-one, even though bondmen, were regularly enlisted. A number of free mulattoes served as drummers and fifers, and as time went on many slaves were offered by their masters as substitutes.

For the reward of such men as were known to be slaves at the time of their mustering into the service, an act was passed in 1783 giving them their freedom, and manumission was extended even to those who had received only verbal promises of freedom from their owners if serving as substitutes for the same. The act providing for this emergency reads in this manner:

"1st. Whereas, it has been represented to the General Assembly that during the course of the war many persons in this state have caused their slaves to enlist in certain regiments or corps raised within the same, having tendered such slaves to the officers appointed to recruit forces within the state as substitutes for free persons whose lot or duty it was to serve in such regiments or corps, at the same time representing to such recruiting officers that the slaves so enlisted by their direction and concurrence were free men; and it appearing further to this assemply that on the expiration of the term of enlistment of such slaves that the former owners have attempted again to force them to return to a state of servitude, contrary to the principles of justice and to their own solemn promise:

"2nd. And, whereas, it appears just and reasonable that all persons so enlisted, as aforesaid, who have faithfully served agreeable to the terms of enlistment and have thereby, of course, contributed toward the establishment of American liberty and independence, should enjoy the blessings of freedom as a reward for their toils and labors;

"Be it therefore enacted, that each and every slave who by the appointment and direction of his master hath enlisted in any regiment or corps raised within this state, either on continental or state establishment, and hath been received as a substitute for any free person, whose duty or lot it was to serve in such regiments or corps, and who have served faithfully during the term of such enlistment or hath been discharged from such service by some officer duly authorized to grant such discharge, shall from and after the passing of this act be fully and completely emancipated, shall be held and deemed free in as full and as ample a manner as if each and every one of them had been named in this act. And the Attorney General for the Commonwealth is hereby authorized to commence an action in forma pauperis in behalf of any person above described, who shall after the passing of this act be detained in servitude by any person whatsoever, and if, upon such prosecution, it shall appear that the pauper is entitled to his freedom in consequence of this act, a jury shall be empanelled to assess the damages for his detention."

After the close of the war slaves rendering public service were often set free by special laws for such cases, as the following passage indicates:

"3. And whereas it has been represented to this General Assembly that Aberdeen, a Negro slave, hath labored a number of years in the lead mines, and for his meritorious services is entitled to freedom, be it therefore enacted that the said slave Aberdeen shall be, and is hereby emancipated and declared free, in all full and ample a manner as if he had been born free."

For Negroes who had served as spies in the camps of Great Britain the following statute was passed in October, 1786:

"1st. Whereas, it is represented that James, a Negro slave, the property of William Armstead, gentleman of the County of New Kent, did, with the permission of his master, in the year one thousand seven hundred eighty-one, enter into the service of the Marquis de Lafayette, and at the peril of his life found means to frequent the British camp, and thereby faithfully executed important commissions entrusted to him by the marquis, and the said James hath made application to this assembly to set him free and to make his said master adequate compensation for his value, which is judged reasonable and right to do;

"2nd. Be it therefore enacted that the said James shall from and after the passing of this act enjoy as full freedom as if he had been born free, any law to the contrary notwithstanding.

"3rd. And be it further enacted that the executive shall, as soon as may be, appoint a proper person, and the said William Armstead another, who shall ascertain and fix the value of the said James, and to certify such valuation to the auditor of accounts, who shall issue his warrant to the treasurer for the same, to be paid out of the general fund."

For the benefit of another black man it was decreed in November, 1792, that:

"1st. In consideration of many very essential services rendered to this Commonwealth during the late war by a certain Negro named Saul, now the property of George Kelley, of Norfolk;

"Section 2. Be it enacted by the General Assembly that the execu-tive shall forthwith, or as soon as may be, appoint one fit person and George Kelley, owner of the said slave, one other person, who shall jointly ascertain and fix the value of said slave and certify such valuation to the auditor of public accounts, who shall there-upon issue to said George Kelley a warrant for the amount, payable out of the contingent fund.

"Section 3. And be it further enacted that from and after the said valuation the said Saul shall have and enjoy full liberty and freedom in like manner as if he had been born free.

"Section 4. This act shall commence and be in force from and after the passing thereof."

In October, 1789, manumission was extended to two Negro sailors of the revolution in this manner:

"Whereas, Jack Knight and William Boush, two Negro slaves be-- longing to the Commonwealth, have faithfully served on board the armed vessels thereof for some years past, and said armed vessels are no longer continued on public establishment;

"Be it enacted by the General Assembly, that the said Jack Knight and William Boush are hereby manumitted, set free and discharged from servitude, to all intents and purposes, saving, however, that all persons and bodies politic and corporate, other than those claiming under the Commonwealth all legal or equitable rights, which they might have asserted to the said slaves, if this act had never been made."

William Lee, a Virginian, belonging to George Washington, was granted his freedom by his master and offered an annuity, or a life support, as he preferred, for faithful services in the war. Benja-min Morris, the driver of a baggage wagon, so well acquitted him-self that he was set free. Richard Venie served in the army of the Americans, enlisting with other slaves under his master's command when given a promise of freedom. He fought in the Battles of

Camden, King's Mountain and Eutaw Springs, all occurring in the southern campaign, near the close of the war. He was in the service at the time of Cornwallis' surrender at Yorktown. Not realizing his expectation of being liberated at the close of the struggle, he ran away, but finally received his freedom through an act of the legislature. There was also a Caesar ———, who, very early in the conflict, entered the service of his country and piloted some of the armed vessels of his native state. According to the following statute he was set free at public expense:

"Whereas, it is represented that Mary Tarrant, in the County of Elizabeth City, hath a Negro named Caesar, who entered very early into the service of his country and continued to pilot the armed vessels of his country during the war, in consideration of which meritorious service it is judged expedient to purchase the freedom of said Caesar;

"Be it therefore enacted by the General Assembly that the executive shall appoint a proper person to contract with the said Mary Tarrant for said Caesar, and if they should agree, the person so appointed by the executive shall deliver to said Mary Tarrant a certificate expressing such purchase and the sum, and upon producing such certificate to the auditor of accounts he shall issue a warrant for the same to the treasurer, to be paid by him out of the lighthouse fund.

"And be it further enacted that from and after the execution of the aforesaid certificate the said Caesar shall be manumitted and set free to all intents and purposes."

NORTH CAROLINA.

North Carolina was not unlike the other states at this period in that there were quite a number of free colored people on her soil at the outbreak of the revolution. Persons of this type were required to bear arms and without doubt many of them fought in the struggle for American independence, both in the state and in the continental forces. In the general division of the army under Washington in 1778, there were fifty-eight black men in the North Carolina brigade. Between 1777 and 1783 many acts are to be found on the statute books which forbade the enlisting of slaves as substitutes in the army, and yet they entered in this capacity as well as under other conditions. A law of 1778 declares that they were not to be deprived of their freedom, promised as a reward for enlisting, if entering the army either in the service of the United States or in that of North Carolina. Up to 1780 they were evidently received as substitutes, for a law passed in that year orders military men no longer to recruit them as such.

During the latter part of the war, when the southern campaign was on and food had grown scarce in this state, due partly to the fact that many of the masters of food-bearing vessels were unacquainted with the rivers running through this section, Negroes served as pilots. Such men were first examined, and if their masters gave bond of good security for them they received a certificate to act as the pilots of vessels running into such ports as Bathtown, Roanoke, Beaufort and Brunswick.

That they did not always receive their liberty for military service without resort to legal aid is made manifest by the following act, passed in 1787:

"Whereas, Ned Griffin, late the property of William Kitchin, of Edgecomb County, North Carolina, was promised the full enjoyment of his liberty on condition that he, the said Ned Griffin, should faithfully serve as a soldier in the continental lines of this state for and during the term of twelve months, and whereas, the said Griffin did faithfully on his part perform the condition and, whereas, it is just and reasonable the said Griffin should receive the reward promised for his service as performed;

"Be it therefore enacted by the General Assembly of the State of North Carolina, and it is hereby enacted by the authority of the same, that the said Ned Griffin, late the property of William Kitchin, shall forever hereafter be, in every respect, declared to be a free man, and he shall be and is hereafter enfranchised and forever delivered of the yoke of slavery. Any law, usage or custom to the contrary thereof in any ways notwithstanding."

The Edenton Whig, published in 1849, gives an account of the death of a colored soldier of the Revolution who died in that year at one hundred and one years of age. This man, whose name was Jonathan Overton, served under Washington at Yorktown. This last scene of the struggle for American freedom was located on the York River, in the State of Virginia. The English, having surrounded themselves with fortifications, were in possession of the place. Very early in October the Americans made a furious attack upon them, which was of sufficient degree to force Cornwallis, who was in charge, to send to Clinton, then in New York, for aid. Some time elapsed before this could be secured. During this time the English commander, although advised to do otherwise, remained behind his Virginia fortification, believing that he could hold out until help came. In this he was very much mistaken, for the Americans kept up the seige until October 19th, 1781. By this time, hard pressed and uncertain as to the time of arrival of the forces from the north, Cornwallis held out a flag of truce to Washington, and a little later surrendered his army of seven thousand men as prisoners of war to the Amerian leader. It is said that one black patriot who helped to bring about this victory and who was an eye witness to the scene, remarked jocosely that "Cornwallis would be better called Cobwallis in the future, as the Americans had about knocked off all the kernels (colonels)."

SOUTH CAROLINA.

For the defense and security of the state, South Carolina, in 1775, provided, by a resolution of her General Assembly, for the use of slaves in the army for one year. They might be employed by colonels of regiments as pioneers, laborers and in any other capacity required. Seven shillings and sixpence were allowed to be paid for the services of each slave while actually employed. A little later a resolution was adopted by the same body which forbade the use of the slave in the war, in any capacity, under any condition. This brought about the emancipation of many Negroes that they might enter the service, where their conduct was such that they often received great praise.

The Defense of Fort Moultrie.

Early in 1776 it was decided to fortify Charleston against a probable attack from the enemy's guns. Negroes were drilled in ex-tinguishing fires, placing ladders and in meeting other emergencies that would arise were the city to be shelled. They (Negroes) took lead from the roofs of houses and churches and melted it into bul-lets that the supply of ammunition might be increased. As the city is near the sea it was necessary to place defenses about the harbor by which it is approached. It was therefore decided to erect breast-works on Sullivan's Island, in Charleston Harbor. This piece of land is a low, sandy bar on the right of the inlet. At the time of the war it was covered with marshes, thickets and many trees. This point was selected because it had a deeper channel than that made by the other islands in the neighborhood, and because the British ships were sure to pass that way if they made an effort to storm the city. A fort put up here was laid out in four bastiles. A fascine battery was also erected. Most of this work was done by Negroes, a large force being called in from the outlying plantations. Under the direction of Col. Moultrie "these men ably assisted the whites." They dovetailed the spongy palmetto, whose bullet resisting power is so well known, into a number of pens, connected with each other.

These were filled with sand, making a parapet sixteen feet thick and high enough to shield the defenders and their guns. By April 26 one hundred guns were in operation.

On May 31st the expected British fleet, after having made several unsuccessful attacks off the coast of Virginia and North Carolina, appeared twenty miles off the mouth of the Ashley River. This was followed by some weeks of extra preparation on the part of the Charlestonians. The defenses were attacked on the fifteen of June, at which time a division of Clinton's force opened fire upon the fort, where the Negroes were still at work even when the action began. In the city the blacks, who had been previously trained, took charge of the fire apparatus. So furious was the assault of the Americans that at no time were Clinton's men able to land upon Sullivan or Fort Moultrie, as the point was afterward called. An advance guard of some eight hundred men of both races defended the island at its lower extremity, while there was a force of four hundred and thirty-five in the fort. It was Clinton's plan to proceed to Charleston from this point, but neither the first nor the second division of the British fleet ever effected a landing. Badly crippled, they sailed away up the coast toward New York, where a large force of George III was concentrating. This victory brought security to South Carolina and to Georgia for the next three years. "Much of it, if not most of it, was due the efforts of Negroes."

An effort to Raise a Large Body of Negro Troops.

In March, 1779, Henry Laurens, of this state, wrote the following letter to Washington on the subject of using black men in the army:

"Our affairs in the Southern Department are more favorable than we had considered them a few days ago. Nevertheless, the country is greatly distressed and will be more so unless reinforcements are sent to its relief. Had we arms for three thousand black men such as I could select from Carolina, I should have no doubt of success in driving the British out of Georgia and subduing East Florida before the end of July."

This was a request for the raising of a large body of Negro soldiers. Secretary of Treasury Hamilton approved of this plan, saying that he believed "that the Negroes would make excellent soldiers with proper management." Congress, to whom the matter was referred, considered it of great importance, and appointed a special committee to deliberate upon it. This body recommended that the states of South Carolina and Georgia, if they shall think the same expedient, take measures immediately for the raising of three thousand able-bodied Negroes. These men, Congress further advised, should be formed in a separate corps and battalion according to the arrangements adopted for the main army which should be commanded by white commissioned and noncommissioned officers. It was also resolved that Congress should pay to the owners of such Negroes as should be enlisted full compensation for the same, not exceeding one thousand dollars, for each able-bodied Negro man of standard size and less than thirty-five years of age. The Negroes were not to receive pay or bounty, but were to be clothed and supported by the United States. Those who served well to the end of the war were to return their arms, receive fifty dollars and their emancipation. Col. George Laurens, a son of the man whose request had called forth these resolutions, went home to South Carolina as soon as they were made known, hoping that he might arouse sentiment sufficient to bring about their materialization. Meanwhile Cornwallis, Clinton and Provost were encouraging the slaves to enter the ministerial ranks with the promise of freedom, and they were responding in no small number.* In 1780 Gen. Lin-

---

*Jefferson said the Americans lost twenty thousand of their slaves to the British.

coln also asked that the army of the Continentals be augmented by black men, saying in a letter, "I think the measure of raising a black corps a necessary one. I have great reason to believe if permission is given for it that many men would soon be obtained. I have repeatedly urged this matter not only because Congress has recommended it and because it becomes my duty to attempt to have it executed, but because my own mind suggests the utility and importance of the measure as the safety of the town (Charleston) makes it necessary." This letter was written after the reduction of Charleston by the British under Clinton.

It was in January, 1782, that Gen. Greene wrote the following communication to Washington anent the same matter: "I have recommended to this state to raise some black regiments. To fill up the regiments with whites is impracticable, and to get reinforcements from the northward precarious and at least difficult from the prejudices respecting the climate. Some are for it, but the greater part of the people are opposed to it." To the governor of South Carolina he wrote in part: "The national strength of the country, in point of numbers, it seems to me to consist much more in the blacks than in the whites. Could they be incorporated and employed for its defense it would double your security. That they would make good soldiers I have not the least doubt, and I am persuaded that the state has it not in its power to give sufficient reinforcements without incorporating them either to secure the country, if the enemy mean to act vigorously upon an offensive plan, or to furnish a force sufficient to dispossess them at Charleston should it be defensive. The number of whites in this state is too small, and the state of your finances too low, to raise a force in any other way. Should the measure be adopted it may prove a good means of preventing the enemy from further attempts upon this country when they find they not only have the whites but the blacks also to contend with. And I believe it is generally agreed that if the national strength of this country could have been employed in its defense the enemy would have found it a little less impracticable to have gotten a footing here, much more to have overrun the country, by which the inhabitants have suffered infinitely greater loss than would have been sufficient to have given you perfect security, and I am persuaded the incorporation of a part of the Negroes would rather tend to secure the fidelity of others than excite discontent, mutiny and desertion among them. The force I would ask for this purpose, in addition to what we have and what may probably join us from the northward, or from the militia of this state, would be four regiments, two upon the Continental and two upon the state establishment, a corp of pioneers and a corp of artificers, each to consist of about eighty men. The last two may be either on a temporary or a permanent establishment, as may be the most agreeable to this state. The others should have their freedom and be clothed and treated in all respects as other soldiers, without which they would be unfit for the duties expected of them."

Despite these requests on the part of military officers for the enlistment of a large force of blacks, and despite the endorsement and approval of the same by such men as Washington, Hamilton and Adams, and although Laurens worked for it most faithfully until the year 1782, the time of his death, nothing was accomplished along that line. In the legislature of South Carolina it was out-voted and the chief promoter had passed away before it was settled in the Georgia assembly, where he had hoped for a more satisfactory termination of the matter. Thus ended the effort to organize separate bodies of Negro troops in the South. They were, however, attached to the southern army until the end of the struggle, and not a few were spies and drummers. Numbers of them were engaged in building breastworks, driving teams, and piloting the army through dense woods and swamps and across rivers. In 1783 an act was passed in this state enfranchising the wife and child of a Negro who, while in the employ of Gen. Rutledge, had served as a spy. The emancipation of his wife and child were deemed a just and reasonable reward "because he had executed the commissions with which he was entrusted with diligence and fidelity, and had at the risk of his own life frequently secured important information from the enemy's line."

San Domingo Negroes in the Revolution.

In December, 1778, Savannah was captured by a British force of three thousand men under Col. Campbell. Following this Gen. Provost set up a form of government in the State of Georgia with Savannah as its capital. This place was at that time an unpaved village, protected on the north by the Savannah River and exposed on the eastern and the southern sides, where, after destroying all the bridges entering the town, the British had constructed an unbroken line of fortifications upon the broad field that extended from the river to the swamp.

It was in October of the year 1779 that the Continentals, aided by their allies, the French, made an effort to take Savannah out of the hands of the foe. Dividing their forces they made several lines of approach, hoping to weaken the strength of the enemy by a division of the centers of attention. The rear of the fortifications was attacked by troops under Gen. Dillon. These men became entangled in a morass and were thereby exposed to the fire of the British batteries from two strong redoubts. Many of the forces under Gen. Huger became trapped in low-lying rice fields in the neighborhood, while two hundred cavalrymen under Count Pulaski made an unsuccessful attempt to enter the lines of the enemy between their fortifications. In the confusion which ensued the brave Pole himself received a mortal injury. So steady a fire was kept up from the well-stocked garrison of the English that the main body of the Americans under D'Estaing and Lincoln were forced into retreat. Into the breach thus made the black men, slave and free, of San Domingo, placed themselves, commanded by Vicount de Frontages. They numbered about eight hundred blacks and mulattoes, who had responded to the call of D'Estaing to enter the French division of the American army. Rushing into the conflict "they saved the Franco-American army from total disaster by heroically covering its retreat," which had been very nearly cut off by the marines and grenadiers under Lieut. Col. Maitland.

These forces did not remain in America very long after this engagement, but soon a part of the French fleet returned to France and the rest to the West Indies.

In this brave black battalion were men, some of whom afterward became heroes in the fight for the liberty of their own native soil. Among these were Jean Baptiste Chavanne, who became one of the principals in a slave uprising in Haiti in 1790. For this he was very cruelly put to death on the road to the La Grande Rivere, opposite the estate of Poisson, in the presence of the northern provincial assemply of Haiti, which convened for the special purpose on February 25, 1791. Another of these soldiers was Andre Riguard, who later refused a bribe of three million francs. This sum was offered him by the English, who were operating in the isle of San Domingo in 1794, and whose military bases had been more than once successfully stormed by the forces under Riguard. This made him, of course, a very desirable ally, for all through the stormy period that produced the Negro republic of Haiti he was extremely active. In 1799 he was elected a deputy to their Legislative Assembly. By 1800 he had secured the displeasure of Touissant, who feared him as a rival. For that reason the former fled in a Danish ship to St. Thomas. He reached France, the land for which he had set out, a year later, in the meanwhile having been captured and imprisoned on the Island of St. Christopher by the Americans, who were at that time friendly to the first president of the black republic. He remained in France for some years. In 1810 he returned to Haiti and without bloodshed set up a government independent of the president's in the southern part of the island. This concession came to an end when he died, in Cayes, on September 17, 1811. Others of the volunteers who saved the day at Savannah for the Americans were Beauvais, Martial Besse, Jaurdain, Lambert, Christophe, Morne, Villet, Toureaux, Cange, Leveille, Monsieur Belley and Monsieur Beauregard. On this occasion Beauregard received a severe wound in the hip, which made him a cripple for life. In the engagement he stood near Pulaski and saw him fall. His last days were spent in South Carolina, where he died at an advanced age.

GEORGIA.

Like South Carolina, Georgia was a colony of plantations, on which many Negroes rendered efficient service. Some of these, as elsewhere, did pioneer work in the American Revolution. As early as November, 1776, the slaves of Gov. Wright were, by order of the Council of Safety, directed to build a battery on the Tybee River. These men are spoken of as "able ax men." On another occasion Negroes of the same plantation erected a strong fort and all of the slaves and twenty white men were there armed in its defense. About this time Negroes were employed to repair the causeway of Great Ogechee Ferry. A resolution of the house of the assembly in Savannah, Georgia, May, 1778, empowered the governor to draft from confiscated estates of Loyalists two hundred able-bodied slaves for the use of the Continental army, to act as pioneers in the expedition against East Florida, and one hundred more for the use of the militia and state forces in the same expedition. These men were to do fatigue duty. Trustees were appointed to take charge of the estates and to see that these slaves were furnished for duty. Until these men were available divisions of the army marching into Georgia to join the governor of the state from South Carolina had the bad roads over which they passed repaired by Negroes from neighboring plantations. It became necessary to use force to separate the slaves from their Loyalist masters, and a resolution of the executive council ordered captains whose militia companies were in districts in which there were confiscated estates to bring the required blacks to Savannah. State records reveal the fact that until the war closed these men saw service of various grades with the military corps to which they were assigned.

NEGROES IN THE UNITED STATES NAVY DURING THE REVOLUTION.

At the outbreak of the Revolutionary War the United States had no navy. Therefore many vessels, previously used in trade or for traffic, were fitted up for warfare on the high seas. By these a large number of British ships whose object it was to supply powder on this side of the Atlantic were captured. Most of these improvised war ships, as well as the regulars of the later period, were more or less manned by men of color. There were twenty Negroes on the Royal Lewis, a boat of twenty-six guns, commanded by Capt. Stephen Decatur. They were found in varying numbers on the Trumble, the South Carolina, the Randolph, the Confederacy and the Alliance. Among the crew of the latter vessel was the black Joshua Tiffany. He afterwards served in the war of 812. Here also was James Forten,* of Pennsylvania, who, with his mother's consent, entered the navy at the early age of twelve, where he served as a powder boy. On his second voyage Forten was made a prisoner of war. He was placed on board the English ship Amphyon where he was offered liberty and a life of ease in England by the

---

*This gentleman was the grandfather of the late Mrs. Francis Grimke, of Washington, D. C.

captain, with whose son he had become very friendly aboard ship, but always when tempted by such prospects he would answer, "I am a prisoner for the liberties of my country. I shall never prove traitor to her interests." This he said in spite of the fact that he was well aware he might any day be sold as a slave in the British West Indies. He was finally sent to the Old Jersey prison ship, carrying a letter of commendation from Capt. Beasley, of the Amphyon, and asking for his exchange when possible. On this vessel he remained seven months, watching always for a chance to escape. His generous nature caused him to give up his first opportunity to a young friend, who went off in a chest of old clothes, in which Forten had planned to leave. He was detained on the Old Jersey about fourteen months. In after years when urged to request a pension he would proudly say, "I was a volunteer, sir." On the Alliance was also David Mitchell, a free Negro, who had been captured while on his way from Bermuda to Nova Scotia in an English vessel. On being carried into Newburyport, Massachusetts, he petitioned for his liberty, saying he wished to remain in this country. The petition was granted and he enlisted in the navy of the United States. The naval records show the names of Caesar———, a mere boy, serving on the Brig Hazard under Capt. Job Williams; Cato Blackney, a private, who did duty on the volunteer ship Deane; Cato ———, a cooper, of Boston, who enlisted on the brig Prospect, commanded by Capt. Joseph Vesey, and John Moore, a skipper, of Maryland, on the sloop Roebuck. This boat was captured by the English vessel Dragon, and Moore and others of the crew were kept prisoners at Newport for some time.

A Tale of the Frontier.

Sometime between 1780 and 1785 the Staton family moved from North Carolina to a point near what is now known as Crab Orchard, in the State of Kentucky. After building a log cabin, the head of the family returned to his native state with pack horses to bring back the property which could not be transported on the first trip, leaving his wife and children with no other protection than that of a faithful Negro slave named Pete. Two days after Mr. Staton had gone away his wife and oldest son, Jack, were attacked by Indians while the mother was doing the family washing in a spring not far from the house. The redskins, after mutilating and murdering the woman, left her dead body hanging in the bushes. The boy, however, succeeded in escaping, and climbing the steep bank leading to the house, he gave warning to Pete, who was minding the other children. In a short time the trusty black man had rushed into the house, seized his master's gun and ammunition, and ordered the children to proceed ahead of him to the forest. When about half a mile away from the house he remembered he had left behind the youngest, an infant in the cradle, and leaving the children he returned to the house, where he not only rescued the baby, but brought along some provisions as well. He carried all to the hills, where they lived safely in his care until the return of the father and master. Mr. Staton set Peter free and named the infant in his honor. Since then one child in each generation of the family has been so named for the same reason. Peter did not leave his master's roof after securing his liberty, but spent much of his time in hunting and killing Indians. He became one of the most noted Indian hunters of that period.

(Note: The truthfulness of this story is vouched for by W. R. Jones, a banker of Yellville, Arkansas. Mr. Jones is a direct descendent of the baby rescued by the Negro Peter. Chief Justice Harlan, late of the United States Supreme Court, was also a descendent of the Staton family.)

WAR OF 1812.

CAUSES.

In spite of the Treaty of 1783, Great Britain was reluctant to recognize the independence of America, and manifested her unwillingness in many ways that were unpleasant to the young republic. One of these annoyances consisted in continuing to hold military posts on the western frontier. These she refused to pass over to the United States, and from them she supplied the Indians with arms, and for years incited them to hostility. When the Napoleonic wars were in progress she recruited her navy by press-gangs, whom she disciplined by floggings. In order to escape from this severe treatment many men deserted. Often, to secure more liberal wages, they entered the merchant marine of the United States, which at that time seemed destined to rival that of England, to whom many desirable ports were then closed and whose coasts were blockaded by the French. That she might secure her men, Great Britain ordered her captains to reclaim them on American boats. Succeeding in this, her next move was to declare that a British subject had no right to enter into any military or marine service save that of his own country, and that on this ground she could take Englishmen wherever she found them, be they deserters or not. Acting upon this assumption, her warships stopped American merchant vessels anywhere upon the high seas and sent their officers and men aboard to look for and to secure British subjects. The ablest seamen were, of course, selected, and any sailor unable on the spot to prove that he was not a part of the British nation was carried to serve on the decks of his captors. Some of these kidnapped persons were released upon the application of American consuls on duty in the ports where they happened to be taken. When the case was brought up the English always defended themselves by saying that since both nations spoke the same lnaguage it was a difficult matter to be sure as to the citizenship of those they had captured. They overlooked the fact that beside Negroes they had taken many Swedes, Danes and Portuguese. It is estimated that through these violations of the sovereignty of nations (for the chip's deck is the territory of the country to which it belongs), fourteen thousand men were forced to service in the navy of Great Britain. These impressments were made, not only on the high seas, but within the three-mile limit, and coasting and fishing schooners, as well as all other kinds of ships, were robbed of their men.

THE CHESAPEAKE AFFAIR.

In the year 1806 the American frigate Chesapeake was captured by the English man-of-war Leopard after the former's commander had refused to allow her to be searched for deserters. In the fusilade coincident with her capture some of the crew were killed and several others were wounded by the British. Four men were taken from the Chesapeake. One of these, David Martin, was a Negro of Massachusetts. He was an American, but had been impressed at an earlier date on the Melampus, in the service of England, from an American boat in the Bay of Biscay. The captives were all carried to Halifax, Nova Scotia. It developed that only one was an Englishman. He was hanged on the charge of desertion. The rest were reprieved, on the condition that they enter the British service. It was not until June, 1812, that two of these men were restored to their native land. At that time they were returned to the same ship from which they had been taken. The boat was then lying in the Boston harbor. At her gangway they were received by Lieut. Wilkinson from Lieut. Simpson, a British officer. They were then escorted to the deck, where they were presented to Commodore Bainbridge, who said, "My lads, I am glad to see you. From this deck you were taken by a British outrage. For your return you owe gratitude to your country. Your country now offers you an opportunity to revenge your wrongs, and I cannot doubt you will be desirous of doing so on board this very ship. I trust this flag that flies on board of her shall gloriously defend you in the future."

The affair between the Chesapeake and the Leopard caused great excitement in this country. Many international complications followed, and an apology was demanded, but the English refused to discontinue their search. Not wishing to declare war, the United States first ordered British men-of-war to leave our waters, and a little later laid an embargo on all shipping in American ports, thus prohibiting the sending of exports therefrom. In 1809 the Embargo Act was repealed and a system of non-intercourse and non-importation was established in the cases of both Great Britain and France until either or both would repeal the decrees that they had formerly made against neutral commerce. While France seemed inclined to revoke her decree, England evaded meeting the issue. Such a state of dissatisfaction followed that war was declared in June, 1812.

Our country had, by the census of 1810, a slave population of over a million, while there were almost two hundred thousand free people of color here. Most of the latter were to be found, of course, in the North. The free Negro had, in spite of much opposition and prejudice, become much Americanized. In some places he had even the right of suffrage. This was true in five of the original states. He was the owner of property and the depositor in banks. He was sending his children to school in Washington, Baltimore, Philadelphia, New York and Boston, and he had organized one separate church.* His patriotism kept pace with his progress along other lines, and when the war began he responded to the call to enlist, volunteering in large numbers, especially in the navy where, says one writer, who lived in those days, "there seems to be an entire absence of prejudice against black messmates among the crews of all ships."

The battles of the various campaigns of this war were fought all over that part of the United States lying east of the Mississippi River, between the Great Lakes and the Gulf of Mexico. Some of large moment occurred on the high seas. Indeed, this war has not been incorrectly called "a sailors' war." The first year of the conflict was marked by several disasters on land, notably among them being a defeat at Detroit and the loss of many men from the American ranks in a battle fought in Michigan on the Raisin River.

ATTACKS ON WASHINGTON, BALTIMORE AND OTHER TOWNS ON THE COAST.

In the spring of the years 1813-14 the scene shifted somewhat from the northern border to the Middle Atlantic States. Many depredations were made by the English on the coast at this period. There were attacks at Havre de Grace, Maryland, and on the Delaware shore, which were made with the hope of drawing away the American forces from Canada. At last the conduct of the enemy made the Americans entertain great fear for the safety of the national capital, for the forces of Great Britain had succeeded in entering the waters of the Chesapeake Bay. Gen. Winder was then in charge of the military district which included Maryland and the District of Columbia. Early in August it was reported that the enemy had entered the Patuxent River, a tributary to the Chesapeake. It was expected that the English would make a landing from this stream and proceed overland to Washington. To prevent this Gen. Winder, with a force of several thousand men, awaited their coming at Wood Yard, about twelve miles from the capital city.

---

*The African Methodist Episcopal Church, established in Philadelphia, Pa.

This body of militia had been hastily gathered from Maryland and Virginia. Black men were in its ranks. Among them were John B. Vashon, who volunteered in Leesburg, Virginia, for land service, when the colored men of the northern part of his state were called upon to aid in the defense of the country, as soon as the alarm was given that the British were nearing the capital. Another Negro who entered the army of the United States at this time was Louis Boulagh, a freeman of the State of Virginia. Later he was transferred to the squadron of Commodore J. Shaw, and served in the navy until the close of the war.

Effecting a landing on the Potomac River, the British marched in the opposite direction to that which it had been expected they would, and turned toward Washington by way of Bladensburg, a small village about six miles to the northeast of the capital. Here they met the men under Commodore Barney, whose flotilla had for some weeks previous patrolled the tributaries of the Chesapeake Bay, these men being now the only available force for defensive service for Washington. The meeting, which occurred August 18, 1814, resulted only in a skirmish. The scene of the encounter was a slope, upon which a slight earthwork had been thrown up by the Americans. Black men helped in the erection of this fortification, and served also as soldiers and teamsters. Six guns were mounted at this place. The Americans were put to route in this fight and the brave Barney was very badly wounded.

Washington, D. C.

The proximity of the British greatly alarmed the citizens of Washington, and yet there was little they could do to defend themselves. Following the skirmish at Bladensburg the capital of the nation was stormed. The White House, the Capitol and many other public buildings, as well as a great deal of private property, were burned. In the navy yard there were but a few officers and orderlies. Most of the latter were black men, and a few of the same race were on duty about the city. The rest of the militia were still in Maryland with Gen. Winder.

Baltimore, Md.

The trouble in Washington caused much excitement in Baltimore, whose inhabitants felt it might be their turn next. Therefore, through an order of the Vigilance Committee, issued on August 27, the Monumental City was divided into four sections, as follows:

First Section: The eastern precinct and the eighth ward.
Second Section: Fifth, sixth and seventh wards.
Third Section: Second, third and fourth wards.
Fourth Section: First ward and western precinct.
Breastworks were erected in all of these sections. Exempts and free people of color of the first section were called out on Sunday morning at six o'clock to Hampstead Hill, where, with provisions to last them through the day they went to work. This same class of people was set to work at the same hour at Myer Garden in the second section on Monday morning. On Tuesday, those residing in the third district began throwing up breastworks in Washington Square, while the black and the white inhabitants of the fourth district proceeded to the corner of Eutaw and Market streets on Wednesday morning that they might do their share in preparing defences for the city. Owners of slaves were asked to send the same to work on the days assigned to the several districts in which they lived. The masters complied with this request. No event is said to have occurred on the part of the black and white compatriots "to sully the character of an individual soldier." On the third of September the Vigilance Committee resolved: "That all free people of color be, and they are hereby ordered, to attend daily, commencing with Wednesday, the fifth instant, at the different works erected about the city for the purpose of laboring thereon, and for which they shall receive an allowance of fifty cents a day, together with a soldier's rations." Following these preparations Baltimore was attacked both by land and by sea. The battle on the sea was the bombarding of Fort McHenry. It was at this time that the song, "The Star Spangled Banner," was written. A land engagement took place about two miles out of the city, near Bear Creek, on the road to North Point. Beside working at putting up fortifications, colored men were employed in and about the city of Baltimore in other capacities, for they manned the batteries and also carried muskets.

Philadelphia.

Alarmed by the conduct of the foe at Washington and Baltimore, many of the other coast cities began to make preparation for their own protection. In Philadelphia, the Vigilance Committee solicited the aid of Absolem Jones, Richard Allen and James Forten, all Negroes. It was desired that these men should secure the services of members of their own race in erecting defences about the city. Through their efforts twenty-five hundred black men were gathered in the yard of the State House in August and marched to Grey's Ferry, on the west side o the Schuylkill River, where for two days they were employed in throwing up fortifications, for which they received a vote of thanks, tendered them by the city. Mr. Forten himself worked on these breastworks with twenty of his journeymen. A body of colored troops was organized here at this time and placed under an officer of the United States Army.

New York, N. Y.

On October 24, 1814, the state of New York, in its legislature, provided for the raising of two regiments of free men for service in the army in this way:

"Section 1. Be it enacted by the people of the State of New York, represented in the senate and the assembly, that the governor of this state be, and is hereby authorized to raise by voluntary enlistment, two regiments of free men of color for the defense of the state for three years, unless sooner discharged.

"Section 2. And be it further enacted, that the said regiments shall consist of one thousand and eighty able-bodied men, and the said regiment shall be formed into a brigade or be organized in such manner and employed in such service as the governor of the state shall deem best adapted to defend the said state.

"Section 3. And be it further enacted, that all the commissioned officers of said regiments and brigades shall be white men, and the governor of the state shall be, and is hereby, authorized to commission by brevet all the officers of the said regiments and brigades who shall hold their respective commission until the council of appointment shall have appointed the officers of said regiments and brigades in pursuance of the constitution and laws of said state.

"Section 4 * * *.

"Section 5 * * *.

"Section 6. And be it further enacted, that it shall be lawful for any able-bodied slave, with a written consent of a master or mistress to enlist in such corps and the master or mistress of such slaves, shall be entitled to the pay and bounty allowed him for his service. And further, that the said slave, at the time of his receiving his discharge, shall be deemed and adjudged to have been legally manumitted from that time, and his master or mistress shall not thenceforward be liable for his maintenance,"

Service on the High Seas.

Capt. Porter, who afterward became an admiral in the United States Navy, sailed around Cape Horn in the year 1813. He made this trip into the Pacific Ocean on the Essex in order to meet the Constitution and the Hornet, with both of which vessels he had orders to co-operate. Failing to find either of these men-of-war, he made attacks upon British whalers and largely destroyed their activities in the Pacific, securing four thousand tons of British shipping and four hundred prisoners through his operations. Among the engagements in which Porter took part on this trip was that between his ship and the Phoebe and the Chemf. Black boys as well as men were in the service on the Essex. When Lieut. Wilmer lost his life through a shot which swept him overboard, so great was the grief of Ruff,* a little Negro boy employed by the former, that he committed suicide by jumping overboard. The Essex was finally captured off the coast of Chile.

The Shannon Affair.

The battle between the Shannon and the American boat Chesapeake occurred between Cape Cod and Cape Anne, about thirty niles from Boston Light. It was so near the coast that it might be seen from Salem Heights. It began shortly after six-thirty on the morning of June first, 1813, at which time the boats became entangled. A little later an order was issued that the Chesapeake's boarders be called out.† There were many Negroes on this ship, one of them George Brown, a bugler, was told to give the necessary signal which would summon these men (boarders). This duty was usually performed by a drummer and the unfortunate bugler, not clearly comprehending his task, sounded only a feeble blast. It then became necessary to give all orders orally, most of which were, misunderstood. Much confusion and many blunders were the sequence, and after a very short but hot engagement the Americans were overwhelmed and the brave Lawrence and all his officers lost their lives at this time.

---

*This boy was doubtless a powder boy. It was his duty to carry powder for the gunner.

†Sailing ships used to fight with their yard arms interlocked. The "boarders" were those who went aboard the enemy's ship to fight him.

The Battles of Lake Champlain and of Plattsburg.

During the fall of 1814 the Americans won some important victories in northern New York. For several days in the month of August a large force of some fourteen thousand picked men had been encamped on Lake Saranac, under the British Gen. Macomb. During a trip from Plattsburg to Sackett's Harbor, N. Y., the Americans put these men into such rapid retreat that they left behind them great quantities of provisions and were forced to destroy a great deal of ammunition which they could not carry. "A very fine martial-looking set of colored men were attached to the American Army on this occasion." Among these was Robert Van Vranken, of Albany.

While the conflict raged on land, another was being waged on nearby Lake Champlain, September 11, 1814. When it began the enemy's ships were about three hundred yards away from those of the Americans. Starting at nine o'clock, a furious fire was kept up for two hours, at the end of which time the British surrendered. The fight was so terrific "there was not a mast left on either squadron that could stand to make a sail on." This battle was won by a "superiority of gunnery," and a large proportion of the gunners were men of color. Among these were John Day, who was a marine on board the row galley Viper, and stood like a man at his post in the thickest of the fight, while the blood of his associates washed the deck. Later he was drafted to go with Commodore Bainbridge's relief squadron to the Mediterranean Sea. This expedition went out to rescue American commerce. Day was discharged from the navy March 18, 1816. The result of these two engagements was that the Americans regained possession of northern New York. Another Negro who helped to bring about this satisfactory condition was Charles Black, who had been an impressed seaman. He lost nine hundred dollars owed him by England when he refused to serve that country at the outbreak of this war. 'For his refusal he was placed in Dartmoor prison, along with many others of his fellow-countrymen of the same race. This prison was located in a lonely part of Devonshire County, England, about fifteen miles from Plymouth, and was surrounded by a dreary, barren marshland. It was enclosed by circular walls, the outside one being a mile in circumference. It was necessary to pass through five gates to get behind the prison walls, and a reservoir was built in front of the first gate. The prison consisted of several stone buildings, each large enough to hold fifteen hundred men. The guard consisted of two thousand militia and two companies of artillery. During the time when England was seizing seamen, besides whites four hundred Negroes were here imprisoned. Their sufferings were terrible and escape was almost impossible. In some manner, however, Black got away, returned to his own country and entered the navy in time to participate in the action on the lake. His father was at Bunker Hill and his grandfather was in the French and Indian War.

Services of Negroes on Board Privateers.

Privateers fitted out in Baltimore, New York, Salem and several other seaports played an important part in this war, for the American Navy was at that time entirely too small to cope with the foe. Several hundreds of these boats sailed the high seas, harrassing and capturing merchant vessels as well as the smaller warboats of England. It seems that they went everywhere, to the North Cape, into the British and the Irish Channels, on the coasts of Spain and of Portugal, to the East and the West Indies, to Cape Good Hope and Cape Horn, and on the Indian Ocean. They destroyed millions of dollars' worth of property and took several thousand boats. Through their use many American seamen were employed who would have otherwise have had nothing to do, and black men very often sailed on them as members of their crew.

The Governor Tompkins.

In December, 1812, a privateer, the Governor Tompkins, of New York, gave chase to what appeared to be an English merchantman, but which afterward proved to be a frigate in disguise. At last a squall drove the Tompkins under the very guns of her antagonist. In a losing fight, in favor of the enemy, the American escaped only by lightening her cargo and throwing her ammunition overboard. Her escape was not accomplished before the furious fire from the enemy had killed two men and wounded six others. Writing of this event to his agent in the city of New York, on January 1, 1813, the captain, Nathaniel Shaler, says: "The name of one of my poor fellows, who was killed outright, ought to be registered on the book of fame and remembered with reverence as long as bravery is considered a virtue. He was a black man by the name of John Johnson. A twenty-four-pound shot struck him in the hip and took away the lower part of his body. In this state the poor brave fellow lay on the deck and several times exclaimed, 'Fire away, boys; never haul the colors down.' The other was a black man by the name of John Davis, who was struck in much the same way. He fell near me, and several times requested to be thrown overboard, saying that he was only in the way of the others. While America has such tars she has little to fear from the tyrants of the ocean."

The David Porter.

In March, 1814, the schooner David Porter, a privateer carrying cotton to France from the United States, bore a government commission to take, burn, sink or destroy the enemy's boats. When in the Bay of Biscay this vessel captured several merchant ships. One of the guns of the David Porter was an eighteen-pounder, mounted on a pivot in midships. This cannon, the only large gun used in the capture of these ships, was commanded by a hugh black man about six feet high and large in proportion. He was said to be the "best natured fellow in the world," and was a general favorite with both the officers and the men. His name was Phillip ————, and his gun was the only dependable weapon on the ship, because the other (there was only one more and that was a small one) could not be used in rough weather. When the Porter made a landing at Lle Dieu, of the west coast of France, Phillip accompanied his commander ashore and attracted very much attention from the natives, many of whom had never seen a Negro before. Even the "governor's lady" asked to have a look at him, and he was carried to her residence, where he was asked many questions concerning his birth place, his traits of character and the like. Feeling he was being used as a show he sought and obtained permission to return to the boat.

The Battle of Lake Erie.

In 1813 the United States had good reasons for fearing that the English forces stationed in Canada might enter the very heart of our country through the lakes on its northern border. By these approaches it would have been an easy matter to have seized Fort Meigs, on the Maumee River, and thus decided the fate of that division of the American Army under Gen. Harrison, then stationed in this region. To secure the ascendency of these waters a campaign was planned and Capt. O. H. Perry, a young naval officer, was appointed to conduct it. Young Perry had the twofold task of creating his squadron as well as that of superintending the construction of his boats, for the brigs, schooners and gunboats comprising his fleet were all built under his eye and direction at Presque Island, now Erie, Pennsylvania, during the winter of

1813-14. By the tenth of July all of the ships were armed and equipped. There were ten vessels, carrying fifty-five guns. The guns were manned by a force of four hundred men, "one-fourth of whom were Negroes." Perry was much dissatisfied with the latter class of seamen, who had been sent to him by Commodore Chauncey, so much so that on July 26th he wrote to his superior officer, saying, "The men that came by Mr. Chaplin were a motley set, blacks, soldiers and boys. I cannot think that you saw them after they were selected. I am, however, pleased to see anything in the shape of a man." A few days later to this letter the gallant Chauncey replied, "I regret you were not pleased with the men sent you by Messrs. Chaplin and Forrest, for to my knowledge a part of them are not surpassed by any seamen we have in the fleet, and I have yet to learn that the color of the skin or the cut and trimmings of the coat can affect a man's qualifications or usefulness. I have nearly fifty blacks on this boat, and many of them are among the best of my men, and those people you call soldiers have been on the sea from two to seventeen years." Chauncey was about this time on board the Pike and engaged in the capture of Fort George, in the northern part of New York State. As he says, many blacks saw service with him in that engagement.

When the cruise of Perry's fleet began, in its search for the enemy, so hurried had been the preparations, that the work was not all completed. There had been little time for training of guns and the like. The winter had been a hard one and many of the men had been sick. On September 13th the enemy was sighted in Put In Bay with a fleet of six boats manned by sixty-five guns. The engagement began a few minutes before twelve on the same day, the British firing as soon as the Americans were half a mile away. As the boats neared each other the guns of three or four of the largest of those belonging to the foe were centered upon the Lawrence, Perry's flagship. This caused her to lose many of her spars and soon rendered all of her guns, save one on the starboard side, unfit for service. So fierce was the attack upon this boat that she was finally forced to drop out of the fight, and Perry's flag was transferred to the Niagara. The passage was made in a small sailboat, in which rode the commander, his young brother and several of the crew. Among the latter was a black man, Cyrus Tiffany. It is he whose likeness is seen in the painting representing the Battle of Lake Erie hanging in the Capitol in Washington, D. C. This man was a resident of Taunton, Massachusetts. He was a noted musician, having fifed with the drummer, Simeon Crossman, for the Revolutionary soldiers of his native town, and served on the warship, the Alliance, in 1797. When passing from the frigate Lawrence to the Niagara, through a storm of bullets and shot, Tiffany, acting on the impulse, tried to pull Perry down into a seat out of danger. The painting above referred to, shows him in this act, of which he was very proud, and concerning which he often spoke on his return home after the war was over.* Through Perry he was pensioned. He later lived in Newport, Rhode Island, with that officer, and at last died in the service on board the Java at the age of eighty, in 1815. While the Lawrence took part in the conflict many of her men were fatally wounded on her decks. Among them was John Brook, a captain of the marines, who was terribly mangled in the hip by a cannon ball. The death of this officer so affected the little mulatto boy of twelve, employed in carrying cartridges on the ship, that he threw himself on the deck, crying pitifully; indeed, so great was his expression of grief that he was ordered carried below. Upon hearing this order he immediately stopped crying and resumed his work at carrying cartridges. This lad was a favorite of Brook as well as his property, and just before he breathed his last he gave directions into whose hands the boy should pass, asking that he be kindly treated.

As soon as Perry had made his passage to the Niagara firing was resumed on both sides. In a short time thereafter great confusion reigned on the British line, due to the fouling of two of their vessels when an effort was being made to bring their uninjured broadsides to bear. Taking advantage of this condition the commander of the Niagara sailed through the line, having two of the enemy's boats on one side and three on the other, firing in both directions as he went. This was done at close range and was followed by a rapid fire in close action on the part of the other American vessels. In twenty minutes a white handkerchief on the Queen Charlotte was the signal that the English had struck colors. In another hour the entire fleet had surrendered. Each side lost a number of men at this time. The battle on Lake Erie made it possible for American troops to invade Canada, and the brilliant campaign which followed was due to the removal of the hostile fleet. The most momentous event, the result of this, was the Battle of the Thames, through which the British lost the territory of Michigan. It also came about that the Indian tribes, allies to the English, were separated, and Tecumseh, their great leader, lost his life. On his report of this bat-

---

*This fact was stated by Mr. Obed Parker, custodian of the Old Colony Historical Association, of Taunton, Mass., to the writer.

tle Perry spoke most highly of the conduct of the black men to whose presence he had formerly objected, saying in a letter to the Secretary of the Navy: "They seemed to be absolutely insensible to danger." Among the Negroes who played a large part in this victory were Jessie Wall, a fifer on the Niagara, and Abraham Chase. The latter was alive in 1860. He was ninety years of age at that time and sat down to a dinner given in Cleveland to the survivors of the battle when the statue to Perry was unveiled in that city. Abraham Williams, of Pennsylvania, also took a very active part in this engagement. He entered the navy in 1812, under Capt Elliott, and held a position at one of the guns on the flagship Law-rence. He was born in Salem, Massachusetts, and died in Lead-ville, Pennsylvania, in 1834.

The Americans were very much harrassed by a series of diffi-culties with the Indians. These came principally through attacks made by the Creeks, a powerful tribe living in what was then the Mississippi Territory, the frontiers of Georgia, Florida and all of Alabama. The redskins were supplied with arms by the English agents at Pensacola, Florida, which was still a Spanish province. They attacked American settlers living in their neighborhood, and were made more zealous and ferocious in that a premium was offered at the British agency for every American scalp that they could bring in. At this time there was no American army in this section, and the militia of Georgia, Tennessee and Alabama were called upon to meet the aboriginies. Gen. Claiborne was in charge of the force thus gotten together, and under his direction fortifica-tions were put up at various places in this section of the country. Many bloody fights took place between the Indians and the whites, the most horrible of which occurred at Fort Mims, Alabama.

THE MASSACRE AT FORT MIMS.

Fort Mims was located in the southern part of the State of Ala-bama, at the conjunction of the Tombigbee and the Alabama rivers. On an acre of land, under the superintendence of a settler by the name of Samuel Mims, an enclosure had been made of upright logs, thereby making a stockade, in the center of which stood the large one-story dwelling of this wealthy pioneer. For some time no In-dians were seen in this neighborhood. Finally the alarm was given in the month of August, 1813, that the Indians were lurking about, and the whites living along the river's banks, becoming much alarmed for their safety, left their homes and carried their slaves into the stockade. On August 30th there were five hundred and fifty-three souls in the fortification, one hundred of whom were white women. On the evening before the massacre Negro slaves minding cows reported having seen the redskins not far from the fort. Their word, however, was not taken, and the very next day, at dinner time, the fort was surrounded by the enemy. The inhabitants fought very bravely for three hours, but at the end of that time the Indians set fire to the place and drove them into a small enclosed section of the stockade where they were butchered in a terrible manner, neither women, children nor old men being spared. At sunset four hundred of their bloody corpses lay about the place. One hundred Negroes lost their lives in this conflict. A Negro woman, who bore the name of Hester (sometimes mentioned as Esther), although wounded in the chest by a ball, in some way managed to escape through a hole in the fence and, in spite of her sufferings she reached the shores of Lake Tensaw, where, finding a canoe, she paddled fifteen miles to Fort Stoddard, and was thus the first to carry news of the attack to Gen. Claiborne, who was stationed at that place.

All through the year 1813 Indian warfare continued. There were battles at Talasahatche, Taledaga and Auttuse, all Alabama settlements. In these colored men assisted the settlers in many lines of defense. One by the name of Evans, acting as a spy, went with several white men across the Alabama River, reconnoitering in an eastern direction from Fort Madison. In a skirmish, which followed their finding an Indian camp, Evans lost his life.

The Canoe Fight.

In a fixed determination to drive the Indians across the frontier many pioneers armed themselves, formed scouting parties, and scoured the country far and wide. Gen. Dale, an early settler, was foremost in this undertaking. He formed a small party of men to march in an expedition to the northern part of Alabama in November to look for Indians. Finding none there, he proceeded to the southeast and reached Randon's Landing, on the Alabama River, where a free Negro by the name of Caesar, a member of his party, had concealed two canoes. In these boats the men of the expedition were to cross the stream. On a morning when all had been ferried across but seven, who were eating a hastily prepared breakfast of boiled beef and potatoes, shouts from the opposite side of the river warned them that they were about to be attacked by Indians. It turned out, however, that the redskins, who were skulking in the grass, did not see the whites, who were screened by a small bank, and they soon left the scene, but were shortly followed by a small party of eleven others of their race, this time all painted chiefs, who came down the river in a flatboat. Upon these men Dale opened fire, calling upon his men, who were on the other bank, to aid him. They did paddle out a short distance toward the middle of the stream, but for some reason went back again, leaving him to manage as best as he could. Their actions made Dale very angry and he leaped into the smaller of the two boats, followed by two of the seven men who were on his side of the river, and all were paddled by the brave Caesar straight toward the Indian canoe, in which now stood nine red men ready for a fierce fight. (Two of the occupants of the boat had leaped into the stream and swam to the shore.) When within twenty yards of the enemy Dale again opened fire and ordered Caesar to carry his boat directly to the side of that of the foe, which the latter unhesitatingly did, and as he accomplished this feat he held the two (boats) in a mighty grasp. This deed enabled Dale to fight with one foot in his own boat and one in that of the enemy. No word was spoken during the conflict save the orders given concerning the placing of the boat and a request made by Caesar when the general was disarmed that he accept the use of the former's bayonet and musket, both of which were accepted. This fight resulted in a victory for the whites; all of the Indians were killed. Among them were several powerful chiefs. It occurred at what is now Claiborne, Alabama.

The Indian conflicts were not ended, however, until near the close of the year 1814. Had the redskins not been subdued New Orleans and Mobile could not have been defended.

A Negro Rally at Fort Boyer, Alabama.

Mobile Point commanded the end of the peninsula at the entrance of the bay of the same name, as well as the navigation of the tributaries of this body of water, near the city of Mobile. It also controlled the sea approaches to west Florida, and was so near Pensacola as to be within easy and swift communication with the same. Lake Borgne occupied the larger part of this place, the rest of which, consisting of ditches and ravines of sand, was partly covered with vegetation. On the northern extremity of this point was Fort Boyer, a redoubt formed on the water side by a semi-circular battery extending four hundred feet. Here, as soon as report came in 1813 of British preparations being made at Pensacola, the garrison began to make reinforcements. An attack was made by the English in September. The day following Boyer was bombarded by the enemy's ship Hermes, and for several days a furious fire was kept up on both sides. The engagement resulted in a victory for the Americans. Before this was accomplished, however, a charge was made by the latter, under Gen. Stump, and so furiously was it met by the English that the Americans retreated in confusion. It is said that even the leader took to flight. It was then that Jeffrey, a Negro, leaping to the back of a horse, rallied the men by imploring them to follow his lead and face the foe. This act had the desired result. Fear was forgotten and the day was won after the assault had continued incessantly until the 18th of the month. During this time one thousand shells had been fired from English warships. Andrew Jackson gave Jeffrey the title of "major" for his conduct on this occasion. This he was always called, even until the time of his death in Nashville, Tennessee, many years later. Beside Jeffrey and other men of color in this siege, there was the freeman, L. C. Flewellen, of Georgia.

CLOSING SCENES OF THE WAR.

Realizing the serious state of affairs threatening because of the depredations of the British on the southern coast of the United States, Jackson sent from his headquarters in Mobile, Alabama, on the 21st of September, 1814, a proclamation to the people of Louisiana announcing that the general government relied upon them for assistance in its defense in this quarter. This was certainly true, for a circular letter sent out from the War Department only a short time before had invited the governors of what were then the southern states, namely, Georgia, Kentucky, Tennessee and the Territory of Mississippi, to organize and hold in readiness upwards of one hundred thousand troops for immediate service in the second war with England. Sometime before this it had been proposed to organize some battalions of free colored men living in this section of the country for service in the army, but so great was the objection raised to this plan on the part of the planters that Jackson made no effort to put it into operation. He now, however, felt that the conducting of such a scheme was unavoidable, and at the time he made his appeal to the whites of Louisiana he also addressed the blacks of the same place in the following words:

"Through a mistaken policy you have heretofore been deprived of a participation in the glorious struggle for national rights in which this country is engaged. This shall no longer exist. As sons of freedom you are now called upon to defend our most inestimable blessing. As Americans, our country looks upon her adopted children for a valorous support, as a faithful return for the advantages enjoyed under her mild, equitable government. As fathers, husbands and brothers, you are summoned to rally 'round the standard of the Eagle, to defend all of which is most dear in existence. Your country, although calling for your exertions, does not wish you to engage in her cause without remunerating you for the services rendered. Your intelligent minds are not to be lead away by false representations. Your love of honor would cause you to despise the man who should attempt to deceive you. With the sincerity of a soldier I now address you. To every noble, true-hearted man of color volunteering to serve through the present conflict with Great Britain, and no longer, there will be paid the same bounty in land and money now received by the white soldiers of the United States, namely, one hundred and sixty acres of land. The non-commissioned officers and privates will be entitled to the same monthly pay, daily rations and clothes furnished to any American soldier. On enrolling yourselves in companies the major general commanding will select officers for your government from your white fellow-citizens. Your non-commissioned officers may be appointed from among yourselves. Due regard will be paid to the feelings of freemen and soldiers. You will not, by being associated with white men in the same corps, be exposed to improper comparisons or unjust sarcasm. As a distinct battalion or regiment, pursuing the path of glory, you will undivided receive the applause and gratitude of your countrymen. To assure you of the sincerity of my intention and my anxiety to engage your invaluable services to this country, I have communicated my wishes to the Governor of Louisiana, who is fully informed as to the manner of enrollment and will give you any necessary information on the subject of this address."

In response to this call a battalion of two hundred and eighty freemen of color was quickly formed through a special act of the Louisiana Legislature and placed under the command of Maj. Lacoste. The equipment of these soldiers was purchased with funds that came from the purse of Col. Fortier, a Creole. The men were ready to enter the field a few hours after they entered the ranks.

In the year 1814 the cultivation of cotton and of sugar were both American industries in the state of infancy. Although this was true, there were one hundred and fifty thousand bales of the former staple stored away in New Orleans, and there were ten thousand hogsheads of sugar in the city. The cotton alone would have been worth many pounds sterling to the manufacturers of Manchester, England. The Crescent City, then, became a coveted prize to the eyes of the British soldiers, who felt it would be an easy matter to subdue the city's mixed population of French creoles, Spanish, American whites, and people of color. A number of the latter were free, educated and the owners of considerable wealth.

During this period one Lafitte, who lived on an island off the lower end of the state of Louisiana, sent a package of letters to the legislature conveying information concerning a threatened invasion on the part of the English. This intelligence threw the city of New Orleans into a state of confusion because it was feared that the advent of the enemy would not only make Louisiana subject to a foreign master, but would also prevent the navigation of the Mississippi River on the part of the settlers in the West, to which section at that time this stream was a necessary and most reliable highway. That they might consider the information contained in the letters the lawmakers convened on the fifth of October, and after six weeks of deliberation they failed to arrange any definite plan for the safety or the protection of the citizens and their property. Finally Andrew Jackson, who was then at Fort St. John, some seven miles below the city of New Orleans, was requested by the legislative body to come to its aid. Wounded and tired, and accompanied by only a few of his officers, he arrived in the Crescent City on the second of December. Immediately upon being given the right of way by the legislators he began to make plans for the defense of the city "which had neither means nor men, fleet nor forts." At a meeting of the governor and other state officials, held soon after his coming, he pledged to protect the city or to die in the attempt, and he appealed to the citizens to forget their differences, which were many, and to unite with him in this effort. Defensive work was at once begun. All the bayous connecting the city with the river were ordered obstructed by earth and sunken logs, and guards were placed at their entrance. Planters in the surrounding country were asked to facilitate this undertaking through the services of their slaves, which they did. Jackson personally inspected the lower part of the river. There he found out that an old fort, located at Baize, was unavailable for the defense of the lower part of the Mississippi, and Fort St. Phillip, at a higher point up the stream, he ordered put into readiness. Back of New Orleans lay Lake Ponchartrain and Lake Borgne. Both of these bodies of water were considered as probably approaches for the enemy. On the latter was stationed Lieut. Jones with six gunboats and several of such vessels were also placed on Lake Ponchartrain.

A part of the time, during which these preparations were going forward, the English fleet was stationed in the waters of Negril Bay, at the western end of the island of Jamaica. In the fleet were twenty thousand red coat soldiers, among them being two regiments of Negro troops from the West Indies. These men were all animated with the hope of not only taking New Orleans but occupying it, and they were so sure of success that several gentlemen among them had already been selected to hold offices of civil authority. Leaving the Jamaican seas the English came in sight of the American shore early in December. The main body of the flotilla was left at Prue Island, while a small division sailed on and entered Lake Borgne. Here a deadly fight took place between the English and the Americans in the gunboats stationed on the lake. This resulted in a victory for the enemy. Following this engagement more of the foe landed in a wild section twelve miles below the city and surprised a guard stationed at Lake Ponchartrain. This guard consisted only of a picket of eight white men and three mulattoes, who had been located in the village of Bien Benue, not far from the lake, by Gen. Villere, a planter residing in the neighborhood. Through these encroachments the foe now controlled the waters of the Gulf of Mexico. This fact was of course made known to Jackson on his return from a tour of inspection on the 14th of December. He immediately sent orders to Gen. Winchester to look out for the protection of Mobile Point. He urged Gen. Carrol, who was known to be approaching with aid from the north, to hasten, and he made a request to the Secretary of War for a quick supply of arms. On or about the 16th of December the battalion of freemen of color, with a body of dragoons under Felice, he ordered to proceed to the conjunction of Bayou Sauvage and the River Chef Menten, from which place they might watch a road which led into the city on that side of the bayou bearing the same name as the river. This bayou runs near the rear of New Orleans and from its head the Gentilly road enters that city. It (the bayou) also empties into Lake Borgne, which body of water, it will be remembered, was then in the possession of the enemy. Without a strong guard at this point, then, it is easy to imagine with what facility the Crescent City might be invaded by the foe. It was at this time that a second battalion of colored men was raised. Almost all of these men were from San Domingo. They had a few years before sought refuge in Louisiana while it was a province of France, during the reign of Dessalines in Haiti. They had left the island after having unsuccessfully fought this dark-skinned ruler rather than be ruled by him. These men received their equipment through the generosity of the friendly Fortier, and were placed under the command of Maj. Dauquin. In the meantime panic of the wildest sort prevailed in New Orleans. There were rumors of treason and of slave insurrections. Reports of all events were greatly exaggerated. To restore the confidence of the citizens, Andrew Jackson published a proclamation, proclaimed martial law, and ordered that all able-bodied men, of whatever rank or station, race or color, to serve as soldiers or sailors. So great was the faith of the people in Jackson that his conduct had a very salutary effect upon them. There was a review of the troops on Sunday, December 18th, near the old Spanish cathedral in the public square. The entire population went out to see it. The troops performed military evolutions, at whose close each section of the army, whites, creoles and men of color, were separately addressed by Edward Livingstone in proclamations coming from the commander-in-chief. To the freemen of color he said: "When from the shores of the Mobile I collected you to take arms, inviting you to share the peril and glory of your white fellow-citizens, I expected much from you, for I was not ignorant that you possessed qualities formidable to an invading army. I knew with what fortitude you could endure hunger and thirst and all the fatigues of a campaign. I knew well how you loved your native country and how you, like ourselves, had to defend what man holds most dear, his parents, wife, children and property. You have done more than I expected. In addition to the previous qualifications I before knew you to possess, I find among you a noble enthusiasm, which leads to the performance of great things. Soldiers, the President of the United States shall hear how praiseworthy was your conduct in the hour of danger, and the representatives of the American people will give you the praise your exploit entitles you. Your general anticipates them in applauding your noble ardor. The enemy approaches. His vessels cover our lakes. Our brave citizens are united and all contention has ceased among them. Their only dispute is, who shall win the prize or who the most glory, its noblest reward."

Following the review of troops, orders were given for the obstruction of the several canals around the city or of those leading into it. Much of this work was, of course, done by slaves. On December 21st, a detachment consisting of three regulars, eight other white men, two mulattoes, and a Negro were sent out from Maj. Villere's plantation to reconnoiter in the neighborhood of Lake Bien Venue with the hope of discovering from which direction the British were likely to approach. This scouting party went as far as Fisherman's Village, where on the left bank of the lake (Bien Venue) through the kindness of the planters of Louisiana lived some three hundred Spanish and Portuguese people. It was found that the British, piloted by some of the latter, had landed from a bayou on the Villere plantation, about six miles below New Orleans.

The Battle of Chalmette Plains.

News reached Jackson on the 23rd of the month that the foe occupied the Plains of Chalmette and he decided to fight that night. Ordering all their corps' to break rank at once, shortly after three o'clock that afternoon, he was on the march with a force of some four thousand men. Among them was one battalion of freemen of color, those of San Domingo; the other battalion was left on duty guarding the approach to the city from Gentilly road. It was the plan of the commander-in-chief to corner the foe. This he did by making a circuitous march, keeping close to the river, until the plantation was reached. After placing his artillery and some marines on high ground he began battle about half past seven in the evening. His land forces were aided by a deadly fire from the broadsides of the Carolina, the one gunboat remaining on the water. A fierce fight was waged, partly in darkness and partly in the light of a full moon. Most of it was done at close range, and often sharp knives were the only weapons used by the Americans. The battle occurred in plain sight of the plantation houses. By ten o'clock the engagement was over. The Americans were victorious, having lost only twenty-four from their ranks. Jackson was proud of his mixed army and in a dispatch to the Secretary of War spoke of the manifestations of great bravery made by the colored men while a gentleman who chronicled the events of that period as they were occurring wrote, referring to these men of color, "they behaved well —many being men of property, and all accustomed to labor, possessing national pride and constitutional bravery and scorning to be outdone by the whites. They were accordingly valuable troops in our line."

December 24—January 1.

Very early the next day Jackson began the fortification of the river bank leading to the city. To do this he secured spades, shovels, pickaxes, wheelbarrows and carts from New Orleans. All of his men worked, for each company of troops had its own embankment to throw up. They made a line of defenses a mile long, and in some places five feet high. By night the works were partly completed and two small cannon were placed in position on the-high-road. The operations went on through Christmas Day, while the enemy still lurked behind the plantation bouses of Chalmette. On the twenty-sixth of December the battalion of native colored men, under Lacoste, were withdrawn from Gentilly road and stationed at Camp Jackson. The next day the Carolina was blown up by the English. Meanwhile small bodies of American troops in ambush embarrassed the English with intermittent sharpshooting. On the morning of the 28th the British began their advance towards New Orleans. The American forces lay between them and the city and stopped their progress by a deadly fire. On December twenty-eighth or twenty-ninth a portion of the right bank of the river was fortified. One hundred and fifty Negroes laid a parapet there. These black men also erected a closed redoubt in this neighborhood and surrounded it by a foose or ditch. This work was done under the direction of Latour by Gen; Jackson's orders. Every effort was made to strengthen the protections of the river in the neighborhood of the city.

The Battle of the Batteries.

The position of each army had been so advanced through the work of fortifications that by January 1st they were within three hundred yards of each other and on a broad plain not very far from the city of New Orleans. On that day, shortly after ten o'clock in the morning, a battle occurred in which fifty pieces of cannon were discharged at intervals of from one to three times a minute. Often a half dozen guns were fired simultaneously. On this occasion the battalion of native freemen of color occupied the position between Batteries three and four, while from between four and five the San Domingans, under Maj. Dauquin, directed their fire against the enemy. In this engagement four hundred Britons were wounded.

The Battle of New Orleans.

On January 8th came the Battle of New Orleans. It occurred very early in the morning and but a short distance from the city line. It was not long before Packingham's great army began to show the effect of the telling fire directed from the American batteries in this engagement. Both battalions of colored men were on the field at this time. They occupied no insignificant place, being quite near Andrew Jackson himself and operating the guns in Batteries three and four. From the beginning events were in favor of the Americans. The British commander, making an effort to rally his men, had a horse killed under him. Later, while leading in a second effort to rally his troops, he was shot as he raised his hat to hurrah. He received a wound and fell. As his men were lifting him to bear him from the field he received a third shot which proved fatal. His death occurred a few minutes later under a live oak in the rear of the scene. Writing of this event, Andrew Jackson said to President Munroe, who was then the Secretary of War, "I have always believed he (Packingham) fell from the bullet of a freeman of color, a famous rifle shot of the Attakapas District." One or two of his aides fell at the same time that Packingham did. The death of these men resulted in panic and confusion for the enemy. Troops lost their courage and fled in wild dismay. In a short time, save for the wounded, dying or dead, the immediate field was clear. In a faraway ditch were the English forces under Gen. Lambert, who had escaped by lying upon the ground on their faces. For a quarter of a mile the field was covered with the dying or the dead. When the conflict was over the Americans were much stirred by the sight of their melancholy victory, and without asking leave began to render first-aid service, even carrying the wounded on their backs into their camps. Many of the English, not understanding the language of the blacks who came from the American lines, unarmed, to assist in relieving the injured, fired upon them, thus killing a large number. Four hundred of the enemy were wounded at this time. Many were carried into New Orleans and nursed. A few officers were cared for by the whites, and many privates by the quadroon women, who were already famous as nurses in time of pestilence, and who offered their services for this work most freely. For this they received no compensation of any kind whatever, although they faithfully watched by the wounded Britons day and night. Among the freemen of color in this battle was Jordan Noble, the "matchless drummer." In his corps were Adolph Brooks and William Savage. He appeared in the celebration of the Battle of New Orleans at the St. Charles Theater in 1854, in the city of the same name. There was also John Julius, sometimes called Julius Bennoit, who while engaged on the breastworks of Chalmette was wounded in the neck by a bayonet, and there, too, was Anthony Gill. Jackson, in speaking of the battle, said, "The two corps of colored volunteers have not disappointed the hopes that were formed of their courage and perseverence in the performance of duty.

Negroes at Fort St. Phillips.

Close upon the Battle of New Orleans came the storming of Fort St. Phillips. This point was very important, as it commanded an entrance into the Mississippi River. The Americans had made every effort to strengthen its defenses in the summer of 1814. Negroes in great numbers were there employed at that time. On the 8th of January the place was attacked by British gunboats, that kept up their siege intermittently for a period of ten days. The garrison of three hundred and sixty-six held out successfully during this engagement. Its defensive force were' thirty freemen of color, under Listeau. The engagement ended victoriously for the Americans on the eighteenth of January. Meanwhile, peace between this country and Great Britain had already been declared.

BIBLIOGRAPHY.

(In the following list of books may be found an account of the services of Negroes as chronicled in the foregoing pages.)

DEFENSIVE SERVICES OF NEGROES IN COLONIAL WARS.

New York.

1. New York State Library Bulletin, 1898-1902.
2. American Colonies of 17th Century. Vol. II. Osgood.

Massachusetts.

1. History of New England. Vol. II. Palfrey.
2. History of Slavery in Massachusetts. Moore, George.

North Carolina.

1. Colonial Records of North Carolina. Vol. I.
2. History of North Carolina. Raper.

South Carolina.

1. Statutes at Large—South Carolina. Vol. VII.
2. Early History of Virginia. Hawks, F. C.
3. History of South Carolina. Simms.
4. History of the United States. Eggleston.

Rhode Island.

1. Rhode Island Colonial Records. Vol. IV.

Virginia.

1. Slavery in Virginia. Ballagh.
2. Statutes of Virginia. Vols. I, IV. Henning.

Georgia.

1. The Early History of Virginia and other Southern States. Hawks.

NEGROES IN THE FRENCH AND INDIAN WAR.

Braddock's Campaign.

1. Massachusetts Archives—Muster Rolls. Vols. 91-94.
2. "The Gazette," published in Lancaster, Ohio, February, 1843.
3. History of Cumberland, Md. Lowdermilk.
4. History of Washington County (Md.). Hager.
5. Washington and Braddock Expedition, The. Haddock.
6. History of Buck County, Pa.
7. Virginia. Campbell.

The Surrender of Fort DuQuesne.

1. Provincial History of Pennsylvania. Balch.

Raids.

1. The History of Cumberland (Md.). Lowdermilk.

Northern Campaign.

1. The French and Indian War—Muster Rolls of Massachusetts. Vols. 97, 98.
2. Indians in Their Wars with White People.
3. Patriots of American Revolution. Nell, Wm.
4. Slavery in New Jersey. Cooley.
5. The French and Indian War. Johnson.

The Story of Crispus Attucks.

1. History of the United States. Botta.
2. The American Revolution. Hawks.
3. History of the United States. Vol. VI. Bancroft.
4. An Historical Research. Livermore.
5. Patriots of the American Revolution. Nell.
6. Adam's Works. Vol. II.

Massachusetts.
1. Soldiers and Sailors of the Revolution. Vols. II, III, IX.
2. Groton During the Revolution. S. A. Green.
3. Massachusetts Archives. Vol. XXX.
4. "Objects of Interest" (a catalog of Old Colony Hist. Asso.).
Vermont.
Slavery in Massachusetts. Moore.
New Hampshire.
1. Patriots of the American Revolution. Nell.
2. Muster Rolls of New Hampshire.
Rhode Island.
1. The Defence of Fort Mercer.
2. Revolutionary Papers. Vol. 199, Mass. Archives.
3. History of Rhode Island. Vol. I. Arnold.
4. An Historical Research. Livermore.
5. American Patriots. Nell, W. C.
6. An Historical Inquiry. Ryder.
7. Military Journal. Thatcher.
8. American Revolution—Frank Moore's Diary of.
Connecticut.
1. Slavery in Connecticut. Steiner.
2. Patriots of the American Revolution. Nell, W. C.
New York.
1. Field Book of the American Revolution. Lossing.
2. Our Country. Lossing.
3. American Archives. 5th Series, Vol. I. Force.
4. New York in the Revolution. Fernow.
5. Camp Fires of Afro-Americans. Wilson.
6. American Patriots of the Revolution. Nell, W. C.
New Jersey.
1. History of the United States. Vol. V. Bancroft.
2. Assembly Journal (N. J.). 8th Sess., 2d Sit., Aug. 3-Sept. 1, 1784.
3. Slavery in New Jersey in Johns Hopkins' Historic Studies. Vol. XIV.
Pennsylvania.
Minutes of Supreme Executive Council. Vol. II.
Maryland.
1. An Historical Research. Moore, George.
2. Slavery in Maryland. Bracket.
Virginia.
1. American Archives. 4th Series, Vol. III. Force.
2. Statutes of Virginia. Vols. IX, XI, XIII. Hening.
3. Slavery in Virginia. Ballagh.
North Carolina.
1. Laws of North Carolina. Vol. XXIV.
2. Slavery in North Carolina. Bassett.
3. American Patriots of the Revolution. W. C. Nell.
South Carolina.
1. American Archives. Series 4, Vol. IV. Force.
2. American Revolution, The. Book 6. Botta.
3. History of South Carolina. Simms.
4. American Revolution, The. Leeky.
5. Speech of Pinkney in U. S. Congress.
6. Life of Washington. Vol. I. Sparks.
7. Correspondence of the American Revolution. Vol. II. Sparks.
8. Life of Green. Vol. II. Johnson.

NEGROES IN THE AMERICAN REVOLUTION.
Georgia.
1. Revolutionary Papers of Georgia. Vols. I, II.
NEGROES IN THE NAVY.
1. The Black Phalanx.
2. Revolutionary Council Papers in Massachusetts State House. Vol. 169.
3. Massachusetts Soldiers and Sailors of the Revolution. Vol. III.
THE WAR OF 1812.
Causes.
1. The War of 1812. Lossing.
Attacks at Bladenburg, Washington and Baltimore.
1. Naval History. Vol. II. Cooper.
2. Loyalty and Devotion of the Colored American in the War of 1812.
Nell. W. C.
3. Niles' Weekly Register. Vol. VII.
4. Citizen Soldiers of Baltimore. Sallafell.
The Shannon.
1. Naval History. Vol. II. Cooper.
Privateers.
Niles' Weekly Register. Vol. V.
History of the War of 1812, The. Johnson, R.
History of American Privateers. Coggeshall.
The Battle of Lake Erie.
Niles' Weekly Register. Vol. VII.
The War of 1812. Lossing.
The Catalog of the Old Colony Historical Association.
Fort Mims.
Niles' Weekly Register. Vol. V.
History of Alabama. Vol. II. Picket.
Life of Jackson. Vol. I. Parton.
Fort Boyer.
1. Loyalty and Devotion of the Colored American in the War of 1812.
Nell, W. C.
The Battles of Chalmette Plains, The Batteries and of New Orleans.
1. Niles' Weekly Register. Vol. VII.
2. Historical Memoir. Latour.
3. Life of Jackson. Vol. II. Parton.
4. Diary of a Louisiana Gentleman. Walker.
5. Louisiana Historical Publications.
6. American People. Sharp.

INDEX.